TOP **10**
CAPE TOWN
& THE WINELANDS

PHILIP BRIGGS

D1347008

DK

EYEWITNESS TRAVEL

Left **Two Oceans Aquarium** Centre **Artwork, Greenmarket Square** Right **Boschendal Wine Estate**

LONDON, NEW YORK,
MELBOURNE, MUNICH AND DELHI
www.dk.com

Design, Editorial and Picture Research, by
Quadrum Solutions, Krishnamai, 33B, Sir
Pochkanwala Road, Worli, Mumbai, India.

Printed and bound in China by
Leo Paper Products Ltd.

First published in Great Britain in 2008
by Dorling Kindersley Limited
80 Strand, London WC2R 0RL
A Penguin Random House Company

15 16 17 10 9 8 7 6 5 4 3

Reprinted with revisions 2010, 2014
Copyright 2008, 2014 © Dorling
Kindersley Limited, London

A CIP catalogue record is available from the
British Library.

ISBN 978 1 4093 2668 7

Within each Top 10 list in this book, no
hierarchy of quality or popularity is implied.
All 10 are, in the editor's opinion, of roughly
equal merit.

MIX
Paper from
responsible sources
FSC
www.fsc.org   FSC™ C018179

Contents

Cape Town & the Winelands' Top 10

The information in this DK Eyewitness Top 10 Travel Guide is checked regularly.

Every effort has been made to ensure that this book is as up-to-date as possible at the time of
going to press. Some details, however, such as telephone numbers, opening hours, prices,
gallery hanging arrangements and travel information are liable to change. The publishers
cannot accept responsibility for any consequences arising from the use of this book, nor for
any material on third party websites, and cannot guarantee that any website address in this
book will be a suitable source of travel information. We value the views and suggestions of
our readers very highly. Please write to: Publisher, DK Eyewitness Travel Guides,
Dorling Kindersley, 80 Strand, London WC2R 0RL, or email: travelguides@dk.com.

Left **Cape Dutch architecture of the Rhenish Complex** Right **Clifton Beach**

Left **Beach huts at False Bay, the Cape Peninsula** Right **A surfer riding the waves in Cape Town**

Key to abbreviations
Adm admission charge payable

CAPE TOWN & THE WINELANDS' TOP 10

CAPE TOWN & THE WINELANDS' TOP 10

TOP 10 Cape Town & the Winelands' Highlights

Modern visitors would agree with Sir Francis Drake's testament to the Cape region as "the fairest Cape in the whole circumference of the earth". Cape Town, sandwiched between the imperious heights of Table Mountain and the blue depths of the Atlantic, has a sensational setting. With its Mediterranean climate, the city is a haven for outdoor enthusiasts, offering hiking opportunities along the spine of the Cape Peninsula, local wildlife to glimpse, lush winelands to explore and pristine beaches on which to relax. For visitors inclined towards cultural pursuits, Cape Town has a vibrant Afro-fusion cultural scene, a rich sense of history and eye-catching colonial architecture.

The Company's Garden

Overshadowed by majestic Table Mountain, this park was established by the first Dutch settlers in 1652 and features an eclectic mix of museums and galleries *(see pp8–9)*.

The V&A Waterfront

Outdoor cafés, a vibrant nightlife and exciting shopping can be enjoyed at this waterfront complex. It is also the departure point for trips to Robben Island *(see pp10–11)*.

District Six Museum

This stirring Cape Town museum documents the apartheid-era evictions of "non-whites" from the central suburb of District Six to the remote Cape Flats *(see pp14–15)*.

Castle of Good Hope

Constructed in the 1670s, South Africa's oldest extant building now houses several museums. The ramparts of the castle overlook the Grand Parade, where rapturous crowds gathered to greet Nelson Mandela on his release from jail in 1990 *(see pp16–17)*.

Milnerton

Cape Town
see map below

Clifton Bay
Table Mountain 5

Pinelands

Kirstenbosch National Botanical Garden 6

Constantia

Groot Constantia Wine Estate 7

Bergvli

Chapman's Point

Noordhoek

Muizenberg

Kommetjie

Fish Hoek

Glencairn

Simon's Town 8

Table Mountain National Park

Cape of Good Hope 9

Preceding pages **The V&A Waterfront**

5 Table Mountain

The thrilling aerial ascent of magnificent Table Mountain leads to a succession of stunning views over the Cape Peninsula and the Winelands (see pp18–19).

6 Kirstenbosch National Botanical Garden

At its best during the spring wildflower season, this garden protects the floral wealth of the Western Cape and is a year-round visitor attraction (see pp20–21).

7 Groot Constantia Wine Estate

South Africa's oldest estate, Groot Constantia is noted for its old-world Cape Dutch architecture nestled amongst leafy vineyards (see pp22–3).

8 Simon's Town and Boulders Beach

All quaint Victorian façades overlooking the splendid False Bay, this sleepy naval town is famed for the comical colony of penguins that waddles around on nearby Boulders Beach (see pp24–5).

10 Stellenbosch

Despite its wealth of impressive Cape Dutch architecture, South Africa's second-oldest town is better known – and justifiably so – as the most central base for exploring the renowned Cape Winelands (see pp28–9).

9 Cape of Good Hope

Pink-hued proteas, grazing antelope and mischievous baboons can be observed at the peninsula's southern tip, where a clifftop lighthouse offers spectacular bird's-eye views over Cape Point (see pp26–7).

TOP 10 The Company's Garden

This blissful oasis of shade and greenery at the heart of Cape Town is surrounded by the city's most important concentration of old buildings and museums. It was established by Jan van Riebeeck in 1652, just weeks after his arrival at the Cape, to provide fresh produce to passing Dutch ships. By the 18th century, what was created as a vegetable patch had transformed into a world-renowned botanical garden that spread over 18 hectares (44 acres) and exported bulbs and other produce to Europe. Today, the garden is a popular lunchtime retreat for city workers. The park-like lawns are inhabited by flocks of feral pigeons and tame squirrels and offer stunning views of the ragged cliffs of Table Mountain.

Walkway, Rose Garden

🕑 Some museums are closed on Sundays.

🍴 Try the Garden Tea Room opposite the aviary.

• Map P5 • Entrance Orange, Queen Victoria, Adderley, Wale and Hatfield Sts
• 021 400 2521
• Garden: open 7am–7pm daily; free
• Museum & Planetarium: open 10am–5pm daily; museum adm R30 (adults), R15 (kids 6–18 yrs), under 5 yrs free; planetarium adm R40 (adults), R20 (kids)
• Slave Lodge: open 10am–5pm Mon–Sat; adm R30 (adults), R15 (kids 6–18 yrs), under 5 yrs free
• National Gallery: open 10am–5pm daily; adm R30 (adults), R15 (kids 6–18 yrs), under 5 yrs free; www.iziko. org.za

Top 10 Features

1. Iziko Slave Lodge
2. St George's Cathedral
3. Entrance to Old Company's Garden
4. Rhodes Statue
5. Aviary & Slave Bell
6. Palm Grove
7. Rose Garden
8. Delville Wood Memorial
9. Iziko South African Museum & Iziko Planetarium
10. South African National Gallery

1 Iziko Slave Lodge
Founded in 1679, this handsome building *(right)*, once an unsanitary and cramped slaves' home, is now a museum charting the history of slave trade.

2 St George's Cathedral
This Anglican cathedral *(above)* was a centre of political protest during the 1980s, and the site of clashes between the police and protesters. The oldest part of the building is a crypt designed by Sir Herbert Baker.

3 Entrance to Old Company's Garden
Flanked by the Slave Lodge and St George's Cathedral, the garden's main entrance *(below)* has not changed position since the 1670s.

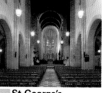

Rhodes Statue
4. Commissioned in 1908, this statue of CJ Rhodes *(left)* depicts the politician with his right arm raised northwards, symbolizing his aim to make Africa a British colony.

Aviary & Slave Bell
5. The aviary opposite the Garden Tea Room houses finches. The Slave Bell is a fire bell moved from Greenmarket Square.

Palm Grove
6. A number of trees in this beautiful grove have labels that detail interesting facts about them.

Rose Garden
7. The site of the Cape's first wine-producing vine and a source of rosewater in the Dutch era, the garden contains many rose varieties, set out in a radial pattern.

Delville Wood Memorial
8. Featuring sculptures by Anton van Wouw and Alfred Turner, this stark memorial *(above)* unveiled in 1930 commemorates the South African casualties of World War I in Delville Wood, France.

Archbishop Desmond Tutu
Desmond Tutu, the first black Archbishop of Cape Town was the bishop of St George's Cathedral. During his tenure, the church was an important centre of the anti-apartheid movement. Post-apartheid, this 1984 Nobel Peace Prize winner chaired the Truth and Reconciliation Commission, and now addresses HIV/AIDS issues.

Iziko South African Museum & Planetarium
9. To the garden's south, this 19th-century mansion *(left)* houses natural history displays, rock art and prehistoric artifacts. Beside it stands the large-domed planetarium.

South African National Gallery
10. From an initial bequest of 45 paintings in 1871, the gallery is now the sub-Saharan region's leading art museum. Apart from its African and European collections, it also features temporary exhibitions.

The planetarium's shows on southern hemisphere constellations are at 2pm Mon–Fri (also 8pm Tue) and 2:30pm Sat–Sun.

TOP 10 The V&A Waterfront

There may well be larger shopping complexes than the V&A (Victoria & Alfred) Waterfront, but none boasts as scenic a location. Sandwiched between the sparkling waters of the Atlantic and the majestic contours of Table Mountain (centre), the waterfront is integral to the modern-day city, as it reconnects it to the sea. The Waterfront complex opened in 1992 and has played an important role in reversing the economic decline that had gripped the historic docklands since the 1960s. Also a functional harbour to this day, the V&A Waterfront is ranked as South Africa's most-visited destination, with a huge choice of eateries, hundreds of shops, numerous sights and several leisure activities, including day tours to Robben Island.

The Cape Wheel

🟢 Don't miss the spectacular panoramic views of Cape Town and Table Mountain from the giant Cape Wheel observation point.

🟢 There are several restaurants and cafés to choose from *(see p68)*.

- Map P2–Q2
- 021 408 7600
- Connected by regular buses to the city centre and Sea Point
- Shops: open 9am–9pm Mon–Sun & public hols
- www.waterfront. co.za
- Two Oceans Aquarium: Dock Rd; 021 418 3823; open 9:30am–6pm daily; adm R118 (adults), R92 (14-17 yrs, students & pensioners), R58 (kids 4-13 yrs; free under 4 yrs; www.aquarium.co.za

Top 10 Features

1. Two Oceans Aquarium
2. Craft Market & Wellness Centre
3. Nobel Square
4. Swing Bridge & Clock Tower
5. Nelson Mandela Gateway
6. Alfred Mall
7. African Trading Post
8. Victoria Wharf Shopping Mall
9. Vaughan Johnson's Wine & Cigar Shop
10. Bay & Sunset Cruise

1 Two Oceans Aquarium
Over 3,000 marine creatures are housed here. Popular exhibits include the "River Meander" with its tame penguins and oyster-catchers, and a kelp forest with fish *(below)*.

2 Craft Market & Wellness Centre
More than 100 stalls in South Africa's largest indoor craft market offer everything from African beadwork to tarot readings and holistic health treatments.

3 Nobel Square
Life-sized statues of four Nobel Peace Prize winners – Luthuli, Tutu, De Klerk and Mandela *(below)* – are set alongside Noria Mabasa's intriguing Makonde-esque sculpture.

 The Two Oceans Aquarium allows qualified divers to dive in the predator and kelp forest exhibits for an additional fee.

Swing Bridge & Clock Tower

A piece of Victoriana, the iconic Clock Tower dates back to 1882. It is reached via a swing bridge that opens to accommodate passing boats (above).

Nelson Mandela Gateway

This is the embarkation point for day tours to Robben Island. It also houses multimedia displays documenting the island's history.

Alfred Mall

Lined with alfresco bars and cafés, this converted Edwardian warehouse (left) is an excellent spot to down refreshments while soaking up the idyllic views over the harbour to Table Mountain.

Taung Trading Post

Shelves of local music CDs and leisure wear are stocked alongside hand-crafted beadwork and authentic Africana items at this craft and curio shop (above).

History of the Docklands

The docklands started to take shape in the 19th century, when in 1860, Prince Alfred (son of Queen Victoria) began the construction of the Alfred Basin by tipping a load of stones into the sea. Despite extensive development over the years, several Victorian buildings on the Waterfront, such as the Ferryman and Mitchell's Pubs and Breakwater Lodge, are still standing.

Vaughan Johnson's Wine & Cigar Shop

Whether it is vintage award-winners or the shop's affordable own-label products, this wine shop (above) is the place to stock up on a few bottles.

Victoria Wharf Shopping Mall

Recuperate from shopping at one of the many restaurants, then catch a movie at the Art Nouveau or Nu Metro cinemas – all in one of South Africa's largest malls.

Bay & Sunset Cruise

You can take a sunset cruise around Table Bay with one of the operators who can be found on Quay 5 and North Wharf.

^{Top}10 Robben Island

Situated in Table Bay, Robben Island is South Africa's version of Alcatraz and has been a place of exile since Van Riebeeck's day. Its first political prisoner, a rebellious local trader named Autshumatom, was sent here in 1658. By the 1760s, the island held 70 prisoners, including several Muslim leaders. Today, it is best known for its role under apartheid, when Robert Sobukwe, Nelson Mandela, Walter Sisulu, Govan Mbeki (father of Thabo Mbeki) and Jacob Zuma among others were imprisoned here. The last prisoner left in 1996 and the island is now a museum and a World Heritage Site.

Church in Island Village

🕐 Arrive at Nelson Mandela Gateway at least 30 minutes prior to departure to explore its museum.

🍴 There are no restaurants on the island, but visitors can get light refreshments at the curio shop.

- Map A2
- 021 405 4500
- Departures from the Nelson Mandela Gateway at the V&A Waterfront: 9am, 11am, 1pm, 3pm, weather permitting; guided tours with return ferry ride: 3½–4 hours • Adm R230 (adults), R120 (kids); book online
- www.robben-island.org.za

Top 10 Features

1. Ferry Trip
2. Robben Island Village
3. Murray's Bay
4. Kramat of Tuan Guru
5. Jan van Riebeeck Quarry
6. Leper's Graveyard
7. Robert Sobukwe Complex
8. Lighthouse
9. Limestone Quarry
10. Maximum Security Prison

1 Ferry Trip
The 30-minute ferry trip *(above)* from the V&A Waterfront is best on calm clear days, with fabulous views across Table Bay. Keep a look out for dolphins and seals.

2 Robben Island Village
Formerly home to the prison wardens, this small village comprises residential quarters for the museum staff. It also has two old churches, the Church of the Good Shepherd (built in 1895) and the Garisson Church, dating back to 1841.

3 Murray's Bay Harbour
Robben Island's small harbour is host to a substantial breeding colony of African penguins *(left)*. The island hosts about 167 bird species, including a significant population of African black oystercatchers that live and breed here.

Robben Island was named after the colony of seals that inhabited the island in the 17th century – robben is Dutch for "seal".

4 Kramat of Tuan Guru

The island tour includes a stop at the shrine of Tuan Guru *(above)*, an Indonesian Islamic cleric, jailed here by the Dutch in the 18th century.

5 Jan van Riebeeck Quarry

The blue slate, used as paving in the building of the Castle of Good Hope, was quarried by Van Riebeeck at the far south of the island.

6 Leper's Graveyard

This cemetery *(above)* seen from the bus tour is testament to the island's role as a leper colony from 1846 to 1930.

Nelson Mandela

Mandela (1918–2013) was the first member of his family to attend school. His political career began in 1944 when, along with Oliver Tambo and Walter Sisulu, he formed the ANC Youth League. Mandela was accused of high treason in 1956, but charges against him were dropped after a four-year trial. However, he was captured and incarcerated on Robben Island in 1964 under charges of treason. Released from jail in 1990, he went on to win the Nobel Peace Prize in 1993 and became president of South Africa in 1994. He stepped down in 1999.

8 Lighthouse

The lighthouse *(above)* was built in 1865 on Minto Hill, the island's highest point. It replaced the fire beacons that were once in use.

9 Limestone Quarry

Mandela and other political prisoners undertook hard labour here. In 1990, former prisoners laid a cairn at this site.

7 Robert Sobukwe Complex

Possibly the island's most forlorn sight, this is where PAC's Robert Sobukwe was held in solitary confinement.

10 Maximum Security Prison

Conducted by former prisoners, the tour of the maximum security block is the sombre highlight of a visit to Robben Island. It includes a peek into Mandela's tiny cell *(left)* and incorporates photographic mementos of that era.

🔟 District Six Museum

Founded in 1994, this award-winning community museum draws on a rich repository of artifacts, photographs and recollections supplied by the forcibly dispossessed residents of District Six. A prosaically-named municipal district, District Six was re-zoned as a whites-only area under the Group Areas Act during the apartheid era (see p34). The museum's exhibits celebrate everyday life as it was in this once-vibrant multicultural suburb, and mourn the destruction that it was subjected to at the hands of the apartheid government. Possibly the most moving of Cape Town's many museums, the District Six Museum provides some insight into the insidious effects of the racial discrimination propagated by the government on the day-to-day life of the ordinary folk who were victimized by it.

Museum façade

🕐 **Many township tours start with a quick peek into the District Six Museum, but it is also worth visiting independently to absorb the minutiae of its detailed and poignant displays.**

🍵 **A coffee shop at the back sells light snacks. Several nearby restaurants serve more filling fare, including the coffee shop in the Castle of Good Hope** *(see p16).*

- *Map Q5*
- *25A Buitenkant St*
- *021 466 7200*
- *Open 9am–4pm Mon–Sat, Sun by appt*
- *Adm R30 (self-guided tours), R45 (guided tours every hour), R15 (kids)*
- *For tours, book in advance*
- *www.districtsix.co.za*

Top 10 Features

1. Painted Floor Map
2. Methodist Church Building
3. "Formation, Resistance, Restitution" Wall Panels
4. Nomvuyo's Room
5. Story of Horstley Street
6. Tribute to Langarm Pioneers
7. Barbershop Display
8. Bloemhof Flats Display
9. Sound Domes
10. Little Wonder Bookshop

Painted Floor Map
In the main hall, a hand-painted street map of District Six before its demise is annotated by former residents with the locations of their houses before the bulldozers arrived *(centre).*

Methodist Church Building
The museum is housed in the Buitenkant Methodist Church, a former wine cellar that was sanctified in 1883. The church deracinated its congregation and merged with a nearby parish.

"Formation, Resistance, Restitution" Wall Panels
Using a combination of pictures, hard facts and interviews with former residents, this series of three wall panels *(below)* recounts the history of District Six since its creation in 1867.

Nomvuyo's Room
This simple exhibit *(below)* re-creates a single multi-purpose room symbolizing the family home of South African author Nomvuyo Ngcelwane, her parents and three siblings, prior to their forced eviction.

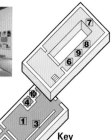

Story of Horstley Street
The memorial hall charts the history of Horstley Street. The mosaic and concrete floor *(above)* has written recollections of residents.

Key
- Ground floor
- First floor

Tribute to Langarm Pioneers
Grainy photographs, period recordings and a stack of 78s by Swing musicians, form a tantalizing introduction to the distinctively South African Langarm "jazz" music that rocked District Six during the 1930s–50s.

Barbershop Display
This cheerfully nostalgic exhibit is a reconstruction of a typical 1950s barbershop, complete with period advertising plates pinned to the wall.

Bloemhof Flats Display
These poignant displays show photographs of Bloemhof Flats, a multiple-block housing development that was built over slummy Wells Square, and was famed for its football team.

Sound Domes
Place your shoes on the marked footprint in front of the mural on the inside front wall of the first floor, and listen to a sequence of ten different stories narrated by former residents of District Six.

The Destruction of District Six

Cape Town's sixth municipal district was established in 1867 on the slopes below Devil's Peak. Its residents comprised freed slaves, immigrants, and people of mixed race. The forced removal of Black residents by the police started in 1901; by 1967, 60,000 residents had been removed to the Cape Flats. The first to return post-apartheid were handed their house keys by Mandela.

Little Wonder Store
It might be small, but this bookshop *(right)* on the ground floor stocks a comprehensive selection of titles about District Six and the many other forced mass evictions undertaken by the apartheid regime.

⏺10 Castle of Good Hope

Constructed between 1666 and 1679, the imposing Castle of Good Hope is the oldest functional building in South Africa. Pentagonal in shape, the castle was built with slate quarried on Robben Island and sandstone from Lion's Head, a small mountain, which is sandwiched between Table Mountain and Signal Hill. The original position of the castle was right alongside Table Bay to protect the nascent Dutch settlement from naval invasion. Having long outlived its original function – the seaward wall now stands about 1 km (half a mile) inland after land reclamation – the castle now preserves a unique cultural and military heritage. Following an extensive program of restoration that took place during 1969–93, it now houses two permanent museums and hosts occasional temporary exhibitions.

Main entrance

▶ If you visit on a weekday, aim to be at the main gate at 10am or noon for the key ceremony and firing of the signal cannon.

● Situated inside the castle to the left of the main entrance gate, De Goewerneur Restaurant serves inexpensive snacks and light meals that have a Cape Malay influence.

• Map Q5
• Cnr Strand & Darling Sts
• 021 787 1260
• Open 9am–4pm daily; free guided tours: 11am, noon, 2pm Mon–Sat
• Adm R30, R15 (pensioners, students and kids)
• De Goewerneur Restaurant: closed Sun • www.castleof goodhope.co.za

Top 10 Features

1. Leeuhek & Moat
2. Main Entrance
3. Block B
4. Governor's & Secunde Houses
5. Kat Balcony
6. William Fehr Collection
7. Military Museum
8. Archway & Old Well
9. Dungeon & Torture Chamber
10. "Fired" Ceramics Exhibition

The key ceremony

Leeuhek & Moat
The way to the entrance is by crossing a moat *(above)*. On the way is the Leeuhek (Lion's Gate), a sentry portal, which was built in 1720 and crowned with two lion sculptures.

Main Entrance
Built in 1683 to replace the seaward entrance, the main entrance is notable for its bell tower made of imported yellow *ystelsteen* and sculpted masonry depicting a lion with seven arrows to represent the provinces of Netherlands. A key ceremony is held here on weekdays.

Block B
The castle's oldest section *(below)* to the right of the main entrance dates from the 1660s. A staircase leads to the grassy bastion, offering superb views across the Grand Parade.

Governor's & Secunde Houses

Part of the 12 m- (39 ft-) high inner wall that bisects the courtyard, the Governor's and Secunde houses were built by Simon van der Stel in the 1690s to accommodate himself and his *secunde* (second-in-command).

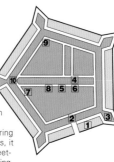

Kat Balcony

This ornate balcony *(left)* has an Anton Anreith bas-relief sculpture. During Dutch colonial times, it was the site for greeting visitors and reading out judicial sentences.

William Fehr Collection

Reached via the Kat Balcony, this collection donated by Dr William Fehr includes paintings by Thomas Baines. Other works give an insight into the lives of early settlers.

Military Museum

The Cape's military past, from the first clash between Bartolomeu Dias and the locals in 1488 to the 1899–1902 South African War, is documented here *(above)*.

Archway & Old Well

The archway connecting the courtyard's two parts is flanked by the covered well that once provided water to the castle's residents, and a memorial to fatalities of World War I.

Dungeon & Torture Chamber

This room below the Nassau Bastion was the site where prisoners were tortured, in accordance with the Dutch law that required a confession before sentencing.

City Hall

Cape Town had no city hall prior to 1905, when the foundation was laid in front of the Grand Parade opposite the castle. The Italian Renaissance-style exterior houses interiors with marble staircases and a stained-glass window commemorating King Edward VII. On his release from jail, Mandela made his first public speech from City Hall's balcony.

"Fired" Ceramics Exhibition

The exhibition features a rare collection of African pottery including one of the world-renowned "Lydenburg Heads", dated to around AD 500 *(right)*.

Table Mountain

South Africa's most celebrated geographical landmark, Table Mountain dominates the Cape Town skyline from almost every direction. This remarkably flat (hence the name) sandstone plateau basks in golden sunlight or is sometimes swathed in the cloudy shroud locals refer to as the "tablecloth". It is reckoned to be the world's most frequently climbed massif, but most people reach the top using the cableway that first opened in 1929 and has since taken over 22 million passengers to the summit. The main attraction of the summit is the fantastic views, which capture Cape Town and the eponymous Peninsula in their full geological glory. The plateau is also an important sanctuary for fynbos vegetation and associated wildlife, and probably ranks as the "number one" day out from Cape Town.

Table Mountain cable car

🕐 The cableway is inoperable on days when mist and cloud settles on the mountain, so if you arrive in Cape Town in good weather, make it your first sightseeing priority.

🍴 The Table Mountain Café caters for all tastes, from a breakfast buffet to a gourmet deli, and is set in a great spot for a high-altitude meal at a reasonable price.

• Map H1 • Tafelberg Road • 021 424 8181
• Cable cars leave every 10–15 minutes from 8:30am–5pm in mid-winter, extending to 9:30pm midsummer
• Fare R105 one-way or R205 return, kids R53 one-way or R100 return • www.tablemountain.net

Top 10 Features

1. Cableway
2. Upper Cableway Viewpoint
3. Fynbos Vegetation
4. Birdlife
5. Dassies & Other Mammals
6. Dassie, Agama & Klipspringer Trails
7. Sign 15 Viewpoint
8. Abseil Africa
9. Maclear's Beacon
10. Platteklip Gorge Trail

Cableway
The breathtaking 5-minute ride seems too short in this circular cable car, complete with rotating floor and 360-degree views of Cape Town and Table Bay. It travels within nerve-racking inches of the sheer cliff face below the Upper Cableway Station.

Upper Cableway Viewpoint
Emerge from the Upper Cableway Station for a view of the pinnacle of Signal Hill *(left)*, Robben Island in Table Bay and the Hottentots Holland on the eastern horizon.

Fynbos Vegetation
A sweeping glance over Table Mountain's sandstone plateau might be your first exposure to *fynbos*, a heath-like cover whose muted shades are offset by fiery pink proteas, multicoloured disas and spectral silver trees.

4 Birdlife
The *fynbos* attracts nectar-dependent sunbirds and sugarbirds. The redwing starling *(right)* and chat often visit the summit. Look out for swifts, kestrels and the black eagle.

5 Dassies & Other Mammals
The Twelve Apostles Terrace is a great place to look for the rock hyrax, or dassie, a loveable guinea pig look-alike often seen basking on the rocky plateau. Other wildlife found here include klipspringer, the gaudy agama lizard and a variety of snakes.

6 Dassie, Agama & Klipspringer Trails
These circular, wheelchair-friendly walks *(left)*, though not teeming with wildlife, offer fantastic views.

7 Sign 15 Viewpoint
This viewpoint offers sweeping vistas over the mountainous spine of the Cape Peninsula, with glimpses of Simon's Town and Kommetjie through the hills.

8 Abseil Africa
A must for adventurous travellers is Abseil Africa's 112-m (367-ft) abseil route *(above)* down the ledge of Table Mountain overlooking Camps Bay *(see p49)*.

Tips for Walkers
Table Mountain has several well-marked trails leading to the summit, which have been graded according to their difficulty. All hikers must wear proper walking boots and are advised to check with the Lower Cableway Station before setting out, as weather conditions may deteriorate without warning. Hiking on windy or misty days is not recommended.

10 Platteklip Gorge Trail
This demanding but popular, non-mechanized alternative to the cableway *(above)* runs to Tafelberg Road from Maclear's Beacon.

9 Maclear's Beacon
The highest point on Table Mountain *(below)* is an attractive goal for peak-baggers and ramblers alike. There's some great scenery along the way, too.

 The walk between the cableway stations via Platteklip Gorge takes 2–4 hours either way, depending on your fitness level.

🔟 Kirstenbosch National Botanical Garden

Kirstenbosch, one of the world's great botanical gardens, was established in 1913 to protect the immense floral wealth of the Western Cape. On the eastern slopes of Table Mountain, the garden is located on land formerly owned by the VOC and leased to Leendert Cornelissen. Later the property of CJ Rhodes, the garden was bequeathed to the nation in 1902. Today, the lower slopes are planted with lush indigenous flora, blending into a natural cover of fynbos and forest at higher altitudes, accessible by a network of footpaths.

King Protea in bloom

Local flora

🌸 Serious botanists should time their visit to coincide with the free guided walks at 10am and 11am from Tuesday to Saturday. Sunset concerts are held on Sundays between December–March.

🍽 Moyo Kirstenbosch serves a range of meals and snacks and also picnic lunch baskets to take out onto the lawns (book 24 hours in advance).

- Map H2
- Rhodes Drive, Kirstenbosch
- 021 799 8783
- Open Apr–Aug 8am–6pm daily; Sep–Mar 8am–7pm daily; conservatory 9am–5pm (6pm summer)
- Adm R45 (adults), R30 (kids)
- Moyo Kirstenbosch: 021 762 9585
- Kirstenbosch Tea Room: 021 797 4883
- www.sanbi.org

Top 10 Features

1. Visitors' Centre & Shop
2. Conservatory
3. Gondwanaland Garden
4. Mathews Rockery
5. Van Riebeeck's Hedge
6. Cycad Garden & The Dell
7. Fynbos Walk
8. Useful Plants Garden
9. Statue Garden
10. Vlei

1 Visitors Centre & Shop

The centre, which is at Gate 1, sells a good map of the garden. A gift shop *(below)* and the Botanical Society Bookshop, stocked with books about South Africa's flora and fauna, are also located here.

2 Conservatory

The glass-roofed conservatory boasts several desert plants from the arid regions of southern Africa. At the centre, a spectacular *baobab*, the largest succulent in the world, towers over the other plants.

3 Gondwana Garden

The rocks on display here *(below)* date back to when there was only one continent, Gondwanaland. The oldest is 3.2 billion years old.

Mathews Rockery

Mathews Rockery has a labyrinthine collection of dry-country plants *(right)* including massive euphorbia trees. It is most spectacular in winter, when the aloe blooms attract nectar-feeding sunbirds.

5 Van Riebeeck's Hedge

This thick hedge *(left)* of native wild almonds planted by Jan van Riebeeck in 1660 marked the boundary of the fledgling Cape Colony. The almond-like fruit of this plant is poisonous.

6 Cycad Garden & The Dell

The garden's oldest part is also the most attractive, with large trees, a stream and a pool set below a natural amphitheatre planted with ancient cycads *(centre)* that evolved 150–200 million years ago.

7 Fynbos Walk

This footpath passes through colourful *fynbos* vegetation unique to the Cape. The colourful proteas found here bloom in winter and spring when they attract the long-tailed Cape sugarbird.

8 Useful Plants Garden

Complete with well-marked signs, this garden has a selection of medicinal plants used to treat everything from headaches and impotence to secondary symptoms of HIV-AIDS.

Wildlife in the Gardens

Though best known for its plants, Kirstenbosch also supports varied fauna, with its 200 vertebrate species. The birds range from the Cape sugarbird and lesser double-collared sunbird to the spectacular black eagle that breeds on Table Mountain cliffs and the francolins that haunt the streams. Mammals include hyraxes and mongooses and two frog species found only on Table Mountain.

9 Sculpture Garden

Situated in the eastern corner of Kirstenbosch, the sprawling Sculpture Garden is scattered with superb examples of contemporary stone sculptures *(right)*, created by artists in Zimbabwe's Shona tradition. Some are available for purchase.

10 Vlei

A wooden boardwalk crosses the small reed-lined *vlei* (marsh), which is a magnet for a wide variety of birds as well as other wildlife, such as the rooikat, grysbok and mongoose, all of which are regularly spotted here.

Groot Constantia Wine Estate

Founded by Simon van der Stel in 1685, Groot Constantia is the oldest wine-producing farm in South Africa and possibly the most famous. It boasts a wonderful setting below the Constantiaberg on the Cape Peninsula some 10 km (6 miles) south of central Cape Town. Home to some of the country's most interesting Cape Dutch architecture, it boasts two gabled buildings completed under the late-8th century proprietorship of Hendrik Cloete. It was under the Cloete family, which owned the farm from 1778 to 1885, that Constantia's dessert wines won international acclaim and the estate became the official supplier to the exiled Napoleon Bonaparte on St Helena. The estate was bought by the Cape Government in 1885 and has been run as a non-profit company since 1993.

Iziko
Orientation Centre /
Oriëntasie Sentrum /
Lokuziqhelanisa

Orientation Centre

🕐 Most visitors dash in and out to see the museums and sample the wines, but it's worth exploring this lovely estate at leisure on foot.

⭐ For traditional Cape food, the estate has two excellent restaurants.

• Map H2
• Groot Constantia Rd
• Estate: 021 794 5128; open 9am–5pm, summer 9am–6pm; wine-tasting: adm R30; cellar tours every hour from 10am–4pm; adm R40 (tasting included); www.groot constantia.co.za
• Manor House Museum: 021 795 5140; open 10am–5pm daily; adm R30; www.iziko.org.za
• The estate's restaurants stay open for dinner

Top 10 Features

1. Wine-Tasting Cellar
2. Historic Gates & Main Drive
3. Manor House Façade
4. Orientation Centre
5. Historic Gardens
6. Manor House Museum
7. Cloete Cellar
8. Historic Bath
9. Jonkershuis
10. Coach House Museum

Wine-Tasting Cellar
Just inside the entrance gate, the wine-tasting and sales centre offers excellent wines. The highly praised Grand Constance revives the dessert wine tradition that earned the estate its fame.

Historic Gates & Main Drive
The magnificent main drive leads right up to the main complex, passing through a gate *(below)* that dates from the 18th century.

Manor House Façade
Expanding on Van der Stel's house, Hendrik Cloete later added the front gables and commissioned the Anton Anreith sculpture in the niche.

Orientation Centre
The orientation centre is a useful first port of call, with its scale model of the estate and informative panels discussing the long history of Constantia.

Historic Gardens

5 Dotted with trees planted in Van der Stel's day, the estate gardens are peaceful and ideal to walk around. They afford views of the vineyards and the sandstone Constantiaberg cliffs.

Manor House Museum

6 This museum in the Manor House is decorated in a style typical of an 18th-century estate owner *(left)*. The furniture and art was donated by collector Alfred de Pass.

Cloete Cellar

7 A narrow structure, the building has South Africa's famous triangular gable and a striking Rococo pediment sculpted by Anton Anreith. Originally a wine cellar, it now displays antique wine storage vessels dating up until the 20th century *(right)*.

Historic Bath

8 This ornate oval pool *(below)* located on the Constantiaberg slopes is of uncertain origin, but it is similar in style to the gable of the main house, which dates from the late 18th century.

Jonkershuis

9 Expanded from an outbuilding, the thatched Jonkershuis (house of the eldest son or *jonkheer*) is an attractive Cape Dutch building with a fine restaurant *(below)*.

Coach House Museum

10 In a courtyard behind the Jonkershuis, the Isaacs Transport Collection features old coaches, carts, bicycles and vintage mule and ox wagons *(above)*.

Simon van der Stel

One of the most influential figures of the early colonial era, Simon van der Stel was born at sea in 1639 to Commander Adriaan van der Stel. He became commander of the Cape in 1679 and was upgraded to Governor in 1691. Van der Stel played a key role in the foundation of Stellenbosch and Simon's Town, both named after him. He retired in 1699 and dedicated himself to the development of Constantia, where he died peacefully in 1712.

TOP 10 Simon's Town and Boulders Beach

South Africa's third-oldest settlement, Simon's Town is named after Governor Simon van der Stel, who selected its harbour as a safe alternative to Table Bay during the stormy Cape winter. The town has a strong historical feel, reflecting its 144-year tenure as Britain's main regional naval base, prior to being handed over to the South African navy in 1957. But far from being the boozy sailors' hangout one might expect, Simon's Town comes across as oddly subdued and genteel. It is lent a distinct character by its wealth of Victorian architecture and lovely location on the steep slopes of the Cape Peninsula above a string of sandy beaches. Most famous of these is Boulders Beach, with its colony of African penguins.

Boulders Beach signs

🄲 The boardwalk leading straight from the Visitor Centre is good for morning photography. The one leading right is better in the afternoon.

🄾 Dine at the Seaforth Restaurant or Bertha's in the Quayside Mall (see p81).

- Map H4
- 021 786 8440
- Metrorail: 080 065 6463; www.cape metrorail.co.za
- Simon's Town Museum: Court Rd; 021 786 3046; open 10am–4pm Mon–Fri, 10am–1pm Sat; adm R10 (adults), R5 (kids)
- South African Naval Museum: Main Rd; 021 787 4686; 9:30am–3:30pm daily
- Visitor Centre: 021 786 2329; call for timings; adm R45 (adults), R20 (kids); www.sanparks.org
- www.simons town.com

Top 10 Features

1. Simon's Town Railway
2. Simon's Town Museum
3. South African Naval Museum
4. Historic Mile
5. Jubilee Square and Quay
6. Seaforth Beach
7. Boulders Visitor Centre
8. Foxy Beach
9. Boulders Beach
10. Willis Walk

1 Simon's Town Rail Route

The Metrorail service *(above)* that begins in Cape Town is one of the world's great suburban train rides, offering a giddying series of beachfront views across False Bay before terminating at Simon's Town's Victorian railway station.

2 Simon's Town Museum

Built as a Governor's Residence, this museum *(right)* houses an exhibition on apartheid's forced removals and a more light-hearted display about a naval dog, Just Nuisance.

3 South African Naval Museum

Situated in a masthouse and sail loft founded in the 1740s, this specialized museum is known for its life-sized replica of a submarine's interior and ship's bridge, the latter with a simulated rocking motion.

It is advisable to only use the Simon's Town railway line during the day or when travelling as part of a group.

Historic Mile
The concentration of old buildings in Simon's Town is most dense along the so-called Historic Mile – Victorian façades that run along St George's Street *(above)*. Stop by the quaint bar at the Lord Nelson Hotel, built in 1929.

Jubilee Square and Quay
At the heart of historic Simon's Town lie palm-lined Jubilee Square and the Quayside Mall, which overlook the harbour. Boat trips launch from the harbour's jetty to explore False Bay and Seal Island.

Seaforth Beach
Sheltered by rocks and occasionally visited by penguins from neighbouring Boulders, Seaforth *(below)* offers safe swimming in calm weather. Its popular beachfront restaurant offers a retreat when the wind gets too strong.

Boulders Visitor Centre
Before visiting the penguin colony, stop at the entrance gate of the visitor centre to watch a DVD about these charismatic creatures. There are also displays about marine birds in general.

Foxy Beach
Reached by a pair of boardwalks, sandy Foxy Beach lies at the heart of the African penguin colony *(centre)*. You can glimpse several hundred penguins surfing, squabbling, sunbathing or strutting around.

Boulders Beach
The sheltering rocks after which Boulders is named make it a lovely, secluded spot for a swim. Although it supports fewer penguins than Foxy Beach, you're bound to spot several between the rocks.

Willis Walk
Situated outside the national park, this wheelchair-friendly boardwalk *(right)* offers opportunities to spot penguins and their offspring, and *fynbos* birds such as Cape canaries and martins.

Boulders Beach Orientation

Boulders lies to the south of Simon's Town and is accessed from the main road to Cape Point via Seaforth or Bellevue Road. Foxy and Boulders Beaches lie within an annexe of Table Mountain National Park and are entered via two separate gates. The Boulders Visitor Centre is at the Foxy Beach gate. Willis Walk, which connects the two gates, is outside the park and is open at all times.

Kayak trips to see penguins, as well as shore- and boat-based whale watching are popular activities on Boulders Beach.

Cape of Good Hope

Though Cape Point is not the southernmost point in Africa, most visitors walk away with the distinct sensation that they've seen the end of the continent, and the place where the mighty Atlantic and Indian oceans merge, such is the scenic drama of the storm-battered headland, whose precipitous cliffs rise to 250 m (820 ft) from the vast blue sea. The Cape of Good Hope (part of Table Mountain National Park) is also of interest for its wealth of fauna, which ranges from the endemic bontebok and Cape mountain zebra to breeding cormorants and passing whales. The Cape of Good Hope has a cover of pastel-hued fynbos (see box on p78), which comprises more plant species than are indigenous to the entire British Isles.

Cape of Good Hope

🐾 Chacma baboons are common in the Cape of Good Hope. Though they are a fascinating sight, these wild animals can be dangerous if you are carrying food.

🍴 The Two Oceans Restaurant adjacent to the car park serves mid-range meals during the day. Tasty ostrich platters are served at the Cape Point Ostrich Farm.

• Map H5
• Table Mountain National Park
• 021 780 9204
• Open Oct–Mar 6am–6pm, Apr–Sep 7am–5pm • Adm R105 (adults), R50 (kids)
• www.capepoint. co.za • Cape Point Ostrich Farm • 021 780 9294 • Open 9:30am– 5:30pm daily; half-hourly tours R45 (adults), R20 (kids) • www.cape pointostrichfarm.com
• Funicular: R49 return

Top 10 Features

1. Buffelsfontein Visitor Centre
2. Kanonkop Walk
3. Rooikrans
4. Cape Point Lighthouse
5. Gifkommetjie Circular Drive
6. Platboom Beach
7. Climb/Funicular to Cape Point
8. Bordjiesdrif
9. Cape of Good Hope Footpath
10. Cape Point Ostrich Farm

1 Buffelsfontein Visitor Centre

This Cape Dutch farmhouse *(above)* should be your first stop if you plan to explore the area. Apart from a stock of books and leaflets about the reserve, it also contains a natural history museum.

2 Kanonkop Walk

A short walking trail that starts at Buffelsfontein, Kanonkop Walk leads to the old signal cannon after which it is named. It passes a 19th-century lime kiln and offers some splendid views across False Bay *(right)*. Look out for the blue disa that flowers here in January and February.

A view of Cape Point

3 Rooikrans

Just 1 km (half a mile) from the main road to Cape Point, this superb viewpoint is the best spot for seasonal whale watching. A footpath leads to the rocky beach below.

Cape Point Lighthouse

Built in 1913–19 with rocks carried by hand from the present-day car park, this is South Africa's brightest lighthouse *(above)*. But the draw here is the stunning scenery, and this seldom disappoints – rain or shine.

Gifkommetjie Circular Drive

This road loop leads through subtly shaded fields of *fynbos* to a ridge studded with mushroom-like balancing rock formations. The views are stunning and energetic visitors can follow the little-used 3-hour walking trail to Hoek van Bobbejaan (Baboon's Corner).

Platboom Beach

This little-visited beach is ideal for swimming. It is reached by a road that passes a giant cross erected in 1965 to commemorate Bartolomeu Dias' landing in 1488 *(see p34)*.

Climb/Funicular to Cape Point

The final ascent to spectacular Cape Point involves hiking a steep footpath, or taking the funicular *(above)* – a rope-supported railway designed for such gradients.

Bordjiesdrif

The tidal pools at this rocky beach are good for marine life and the artificial rock pool above the beach is safe to swim in. Sights include a cross erected to honour Vasco da Gama's landing in 1497, and the Black Rock, an igneous formation.

Cape Point Ostrich Farm

Located 600 m (1,969 ft) from the park entrance, this child-friendly private ostrich farm offers an opportunity to get up close with the world's largest birds *(below)*. It is a good place to pick up ostrich-derived souvenirs, from giant hollowed eggs to plush leatherware.

Cape of Good Hope Footpath

If the windswept ascent to Cape Point hasn't robbed you of breath, try the 90-minute return trail *(above)* from the car park to the Cape of Good Hope beach below, offering stirring views of the lighthouse and good marine birdwatching.

Whales in False Bay

Between July and November, the whales that pass through False Bay can be observed from Rooikrans and other beaches along the reserve's eastern seaboard. The most common is the southern right whale, which typically reaches a length of around 15 m (49 ft). It is also possible to glimpse Bryde's whales, humpback whales and killer whales (orcas). Call 079 391 2105 for news of recent sightings (www.awhale ofaheritageroute.co.za).

ᵀᵒᵖ10 Stellenbosch

Founded by Simon van der Stel in 1679, Stellenbosch is the second oldest town in South Africa, and arguably the most beautiful. Running north from the banks of the Eerste River below the Jonkershoek Mountains, the stately avenues of this university town are lined with venerable Cape Dutch buildings and the shady trees that earned it the nickname of Eikestad (Town of Oaks). This old-world ambience is offset by a contemporary array of restaurants, cafés, bars and shops. It is worth spending a night here to explore the surrounding Winelands; the short drive to nearby Franschhoek via the Helshoogte Pass is packed with must-see sights (see pp30–31).

Display at Rupert Museum

Lanzerac Estate

🍴 Restaurants: see p90.

• Map D2
• Toy & Miniature Museum: 079 981 7067; adm R20 (adults), R10 (kids)
• Rupert Museum: Lower Dorp St; 021 888 3344; adm R20 (adults), R10 (kids)
• Village Museum: 18 Ryneveld St; 021 887 2948; open 9am–5pm Mon–Sat, 10am–1pm Sun (4pm Sep–Apr); adm R30 (adults) R5 (kids); www.stelmus.co.za
• Botanical Garden: Cnr Neethling & Van Riebeeck Rd; open 8am–5pm; free
• Bergkelder Wine Cellar: Adam Tas Rd; 021 809 8025; tour & tasting 8am–5pm Mon–Fri, 9am–2pm Sat; R35 www.fleurducap.co.za
• Lanzerac Wines: 1 Lanzerac Rd; 021 886 5641; tasting 9:30am–4:30pm Mon–Sun; R20; www.lanzeracwines.co.za

Top 10 Features

1 The Braak
2 Toy & Miniature Museum
3 Dorp Street
4 Oom Samie se Winkel
5 Rupert Museum
6 Stellenbosch Village Museum
7 Moederkerk
8 Botanical Garden
9 Bergkelder Wine Cellar
10 Lanzerac Wines

The Braak
The village green (*braak*) is enclosed by historic buildings, notably the Anglican Church of St Mary (1852) (*above*), with its combined Neo-Gothic and Cape Dutch influences, and the Rhenish Church (1823), with a Baroque pulpit.

Toy & Miniature Museum
Housed in a Rhenish parsonage, this museum has tiny houses (right), antique dolls and a re-created Blue Train travelling from a miniature Stellenbosch to Matjiesfontein.

Dorp Street
The best preserved road in town, Dorp Street is lined with pre-20th century Cape Dutch buildings. The finest façades can be seen between the junctions of Herte and Drostdy Streets.

Most museums here are open 9:30am–5pm Mon–Fri and mornings only on Sat; call ahead if you plan to visit on a weekend.

4. Oom Samie se Winkel
Named after former owner Oom (Uncle) Samie Volsteedt, this landmark store *(see p86)* stocks home-made confectionery and Africana *(below)*.

5. Rupert Museum
To the town's southwest, this museum of South African art exhibits works by artists such as Irma Stern and Moses Kotler.

6. Stellenbosch Village Museum
Each of this museum's period-furnished houses *(below)* represents phases in the town's development; the most recent dates from the 1830s.

7. Moederkerk
Opposite the Village Museum, on the site of the original Dutch Reformed Church that burned down in 1710, stands the imposing Moederkerk (Mother Church), a tall Neo-Gothic construction whose steeple was completed in 1866.

8. Botanical Garden
The small but leafy Botanical Garden, the town's best-kept secret, is particularly notable for its collections of *fynbos* plants and dry-country succulents from Namibia.

9. Bergkelder Wine Cellar
This distinctive building nestled below the Papegaaiberg has more than 200 wines. Taste the Cape's finest produce in the atmospheric cellar.

10. Lanzerac Wines
This is the closest estate to Stellenbosch. First planted with vines in 1692, it was then known as Schoongezicht (Beautiful View). Excellent wines and a restaurant *(right)* make it worth a detour.

University of Stellenbosch
South Africa's premier Afrikaans university started life in 1866 as the Stellenbosch Gymnasium in a building that still stands on Dorp Street. The university alumni include four of South Africa's prime ministers (Jan Smuts, DF Malan, JB Hertzog and HF Verwoerd) and anti-apartheid activists such as Beyers Naudé and Heinrich Grosskopf. The town's Botanical Garden was founded by the university in 1922.

Left **Tasting room at Tokara** Centre **Wine from Tokara** Right **View from Hillcrest Berry Orchards**

TOP 10 Stellenbosch To Franschhoek

1 Tokara and Delaire Wine Estates

These estates, perched on the rim of Helshoogte Pass, are best saved for the end of the day, when superb views over the Winelands can be enjoyed at sunset over a glass of local bubbly. ⚜ *Tokara: Map E2; Helshoogte Rd; 021 808 5900; tasting: 9am–5pm Mon–Fri, 10am–3pm Sat, Sun; tasting free; www.tokara.co.za • Delaire: Map E2; Helshoogte Pass Rd; 021 885 8160; tasting: 10am–5pm Mon–Sat, 9:30am–4pm Sun; tasting adm; www.delaire.co.za*

2 Hillcrest Berry Orchards

About 10 km (6 miles) from Stellenbosch, Hillcrest cultivates seven types of berries. Its confections can be tasted at the restaurant or bought at the gift shop. ⚜ *Map E2 • 021 885 1629 • Helshoogte Pass Rd • Open 9am–5pm daily • www.hillcrestberries.co.za*

3 Pniel

Founded by the Berlin Mission Society in 1834 to house former slaves, picturesque Pniel, below the Simonsberg, remained zoned for coloureds under apartheid despite its prime location. Landmarks include a 19th-century church and the 1992 Freedom Monument commemorating the emancipation of slaves. ⚜ *Map E2*

4 Boschendal Wine Estate

Located at the gateway to the Franschhoek Valley, this iconic estate's renowned picnic baskets and wines make for a decadent lunch. ⚜ *Map E2 • 021 870 4274/5 • Open Oct–Mar 8:30am–6:30pm daily; Apr–Sep 9am–4:30pm daily; cellar tours: 10:30am & 11:30am • www.boschendal.co.za*

A vintage car on display at Franschhoek Motor Museum

5 Franschhoek Motor Museum

Situated on the prestigious L'Ormarins Estate, this museum is a magnet for car enthusiasts. The collection includes an 1898 Beeston motor tricycle and a 2003 Ferrari Enzo. ⚜ *Map F2 • R45 towards Franschhoek • 021 874 9000 • Open 10am–4pm Mon–Fri, 10am–3pm Sat–Sun • Adm • www.fmm.co.za*

Vineyards at Boschendal Wine Estate

Boschendal's Le Café is open 10am–5pm daily; the Le Pique-Nique picnic area is open noon–5pm daily from Oct–May.

Franschhoek Cellar

Renowned as a quality producer of red and white wine across a broad price spectrum, this private winery is ideal for serious buyers. It offers wine tasting, cheese or chocolate and wine pairing (by appointment) as well as cheese lunches and sales. ⊗ *Map F2 • Main Rd • 021 876 2086 • Open 9:30am–5pm Mon–Fri, 11am–5pm Sat & Sun • Tasting adm • www.franschhoek-cellar.co.za*

Mont Rochelle

A 5-minute drive – or a steep half-hour walk – from Franschhoek, this small wine estate boasts impressively thatched Cape Dutch buildings. The estate offers a perfect view over the Franschhoek Valley and Middagkrans Mountains, which is best enjoyed from one of the two fine restaurants located on the property. ⊗ *Map F2 • Dassenberg Rd • 021 876 2770 • www.montrochelle.co.za*

Huguenot Monument

A stone monument built on the outskirts of Franschhoek in 1938–48, this monument commemorates the arrival of the Huguenots in 1688. The three high arches represent the holy trinity, while a statue of a woman on a globe displays various religious symbols. ⊗ *Map F3 • Lambrecht Rd • Open 9am–5pm daily • Adm*

Huguenot Memorial Museum

This excellent museum documents the daily life of the French settlers who gave Franschhoek its name and advanced the production of wine in the Cape. ⊗ *Map F3 • Lambrecht Rd • 021 876 2532 • Open 9am–5pm Mon–Sat, 2–5pm Sun • Adm • www. museum.co.za*

Dutch Reformed Church

Franschhoek's architectural gem, the Dutch Reformed Church was built in 1848. Set below the surrounding mountains, the church's whitewashed gables and 19th-century bell tower make a pretty, pastoral picture. ⊗ *Map F2 • Huguenot Rd*

Dutch Reformed Church

The Huguenots

The Huguenots were French Protestants who fled France to escape Catholic persecution during Louis XIV's reign. Franschhoek, then known as Olifantshoek (Elephant's Corner), is a legacy to their influx to the Cape in 1688. Due partly to a Dutch East India Company (VOC) edict that Dutch should be the exclusive language of education, local government and commerce, the Huguenots swiftly integrated into the established settler culture. By 1750, French was barely spoken in the Cape, but the Huguenot influence was a major contributor to South Africa's emergence as a top wine producer. Furthermore, many Afrikaans surnames are of French origin. While some like De Villiers and Malan have survived unchanged, others have been bastardized, such as Cronjé (Cronier) and Nel (Neél).

Left **Foundation of the UDF** Right **The South African War**

🔟 Moments in History

1 Prehistory
The earliest signs of human habitation along Table Bay, dating back 1.4 million years, consist of Stone Age tools of the Acheulean culture. San hunter-gatherers arrived around 30,000 years ago and left a legacy of rock art sites, notably the Cederberg Mountains north of Cape Town. Khoikhoi pastoralists first arrived with their fat-tailed sheep around 2,000 years ago.

2 The Portuguese Arrive
In 1488, Portuguese navigator Bartolomeu Dias became the first European to round the Cape. This led to a succession of clashes with the Khoikhoi that culminated in Captain d'Almeida's death in Table Bay in 1510.

3 Foundation of Cape Town
In 1652, Jan van Riebeeck, an employee of the Dutch East India Company (VOC), founded a victual station in Table Bay to provide fresh produce to passing VOC ships. Within a century, Cape Town was home to settlers from Europe, though slaves outnumbered free citizens.

4 British Occupation and the Great Trek
The relatively liberal governance of Cape Town by the British in 1795 led to the emancipation of slaves in 1834. This so angered slave-owning Boers (Dutch farmers) that over 12,000 moved north in the Great Trek of 1836–43, where they founded Boer Republics, notably the Free State and Transvaal.

5 South African War and Unionization
The South African War of 1899–1902 was initiated by English imperialists to gain control of the Johannesburg goldfields. This bloody three-year engagement led to the formation of the Union of South Africa in 1910, which comprised the Cape, Natal, Transvaal and the Free State. Former Boer general Louis Botha became the first prime minister.

6 Foundation of Apartheid
After the National Party (NP) was voted in by the electorate in 1948, parliamentary acts formalized racial inequities into the ideological monolith apartheid ("separateness").

Nelson Mandela, former ANC leader

Preceding pages **View of flat-topped Table Mountain**

Union workers protesting against apartheid

Sharpeville Massacre and Rivonia Trial

Resistance to apartheid was galvanized by the police massacre of 69 civilians at a peaceful protest at Sharpeville in 1960. This led to the formation of Umkhonto we Sizwe (the armed wing of the banned ANC) under Nelson Mandela, who was convicted of treason along with other anti-apartheid leaders in the Rivonia Trial of 1962–3.

Foundation of the UDF

In 1983, some 15,000 anti-apartheid activists congregated at Mitchells Plain to form the United Democratic Front (UDF), effectively the domestic representative of the ANC in apartheid's dying years.

Release of Nelson Mandela

President FW de Klerk lifted the ban on the ANC in February 1990, and Mandela was released from prison after 27 years. He made his first speech outside Cape Town's City Hall (see p17).

Democracy

In May 1994, the ANC swept to victory in South Africa's first fully democratic elections, after securing eight of the nine provinces, the exception being the Western Cape, the last stronghold of the NP. Mandela was inaugurated as president.

Top 10 Famous South Africans

1 Jan van Riebeeck

Founder of Cape Town, Van Riebeeck was commander of the Cape until 1662.

2 Simon van der Stel

Governor of the Cape 1679–99, Van der Stel was the founder of Stellenbosch and prime mover behind the development of the Constantia wineries.

3 Cecil John Rhodes

British mining magnate Rhodes founded the diamond company De Beers, and was prime minister of the Cape from 1890 to 1895.

4 Breyten Breytenbach (b. 1939)

This Cape Town-educated poet and novelist, imprisoned for anti-apartheid activities, now resides in France.

5 Nelson Mandela

South Africa's most famous son was incarcerated in prisons around Cape Town for 27 years (see p13).

6 Archbishop Desmond Tutu

This Nobel Peace Prize winner served as Anglican Archbishop of Cape Town between 1985 and 1995 (see p9).

7 Brenda Fassie

The "Madonna of the Townships" was a popular recording artist prior to her drug-related death in 2004.

8 Jacques Kallis

One of South Africa's greatest cricketers.

9 Benni McCarthy

This footballer has scored 31 international goals.

10 JM Coetzee

Recipient of the 2003 Nobel Prize for Literature and two-time Booker Prize winner.

Left **View of Table Mountain from Bloubergstrand** Right **Vistas along Chapman's Peak Drive**

Viewpoints

1 Table Mountain Upper Cableway

Within 15 minutes of the Upper Cableway station, a succession of viewpoints reveal the geography of the Western Cape, from nearby Signal Hill and City Bowl to surf-splashed Robben Island and False Bay, all overshadowed by the Hottentots Holland Mountains. No less impressive are the views across the Cape Peninsula's mountainous spine to Cape Point.

2 Signal Hill

Rising between the City Bowl and Sea Point, flat-topped 350-m (1,148-ft) Signal Hill is an extension of a taller, hornlike rock formation known as Lion's Head. Accessible by car or foot, the picnic site affords a stunning view over the city centre, especially at sunset with the red western Atlantic sky. Many visitors like to visit in time for the firing of the Noon Gun, a tradition that dates back to the 18th century *(see p62)*.

3 Rhodes Memorial

Situated on the eastern slopes of Table Mountain, this is a rather bombastic memorial. The views over the Cape Flats to distant Helderberg and the Hottentots Holland Mountains are best enjoyed from the adjacent coffee shop *(see p73)*.

4 Chapman's Peak Drive

One of the world's most spectacular marine drives, this toll road was constructed in 1915–22 along the band of shale that divides the granite base of Chapman's Peak from the overlying sandstone. It winds along the mountainside between Hout Bay and Noordhoek with viewpoints along the way. Stop to admire the sheer cliffs of Chapman's Peak and the Atlantic battering the shore below *(see p78)*. ◈ *Map G3 • Light vehicles: adm • www.chapmanspeakdrive.co.za*

5 Cape Point

Situated at the southern tip of the Cape Peninsula within the Cape of Good Hope *(see pp26–7)*, Cape Point is reached via a steep footpath or a chuffing funicular. The views include windswept cliffs and Atlantic-battered beaches to an open seascape that stretches all the way south to Antarctica *(see pp26–7)*.

Views of Cape Town from Signal Hill

6 Rooikrans

In the far south of the Table Mountain National Park, this underutilized viewpoint provides a thrilling north-facing vantage on the False Bay seaboard. There are great whale watching opportunities between June and November *(see p26).*

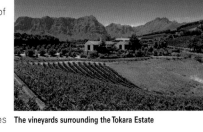
The vineyards surrounding the Tokara Estate

7 Bloubergstrand

About 10 km (6 miles) north of Cape Town, the Bloubergstrand beach hems in Table Bay on the West Coast. This "Blue Mountain Beach" is named after the flat-topped Table Mountain, which looms over its sandy expanse. Usually at its prettiest in the morning, the beach is worth visiting in the afternoon as well, when you can enjoy the vista from alfresco cafés *(see p61).*

8 Tokara Wine Estate

At the crest of Helshoogte Pass, this wine and olive estate boasts perhaps the most scenic location in the Winelands. The views stretch across eucalyptus-swathed slopes to False Bay and – on a clear day – distant Table Mountain. Best enjoyed with a chilled glass of one of the estate's crisp Sauvignon Blanc wines *(see p30).*

9 Franschhoek Pass

This pass is often ignored by tourists because it leads to remote Villiersdorp rather than trendy Stellenbosch. But it is worth following this road for a couple of kilometres to take in the lovely views over the thatched rooftops and the expansive vineyards that are located in the Franschhoek Valley *(see p31).*

10 Paarl Mountain

The world's second-largest granite outcrop, Paarl Mountain is on the outskirts of Paarl. The mountain is at its most spectacular at dusk when it glows like a pearl, from where it gets its name. A 2-hour trail leads to the top of the outcrop. Views from this point stretch to the *fynbos*-covered lower slopes and the bustling town, and extend to the surrounding vineyards and the Drakenstein (Dragon's Stone) Mountain's outline. ◈ *Map E1*

Left **Scratch Patch** Centre **Lioness at Drakenstein Lion Park** Right **Monkey Jungle at World of Birds**

Activities for Children

1 Monkey Town Primate Sanctuary

Most of the primates of this sanctuary have been rescued from captivity. The species, ranging from chimps to the pygmy marmoset, are housed in a large, green enclosure surrounded by a viewing walkway. § Map D4 • Mondeor Rd, Somerset West • 021 858 1060 • Open 8am–5pm daily • www. monkeys.co.za

2 Scratch Patch

With branches in Simon's Town and the V&A Waterfront, Scratch Patch resembles a psychedelic gravel heap. A profusion of colourful, tumble-polished gemstones – including tiger's eye, lapis lazuli, blue lace agate, rose quartz, amethyst and jasper – is scattered on the floor. For a small fee, kids (and adults) can "scratch" around and fill bagfuls to take home. § The V&A Waterfront: Map A2; Dock Rd; 021 419 9429; open 9am–5:30pm daily • Simon's

Town: Map H4; Dido Valley Rd; 021 786 2020; open 8:30am–4:45pm Mon–Fri, 9am–5:30pm Sat–Sun • www. scratchpatch.co.za

Macaw parrots

3 Iziko Planetarium

The domed planetarium, part of the National Museum complex in the Company's Garden, features daily shows introducing the brilliant southern night sky. Other specialized shows include programmes for kids (see p9).

4 World of Birds

Situated in Hout Bay, World of Birds is Africa's largest bird park with over 400 indigenous and exotic species, including parrots and barbets, in walk-through aviaries. Visitors can glimpse the various aspects of birdlife, right from eggs in incubation to the feeding of chicks. The park also features reptiles and mammals, especially monkeys, in its Monkey Jungle (see p79).

5 Giraffe House

Giraffe House provides easy access to some wonderful wildlife and bird species. Focusing on African wildlife, the sanctuary provides an amazing opportunity to enjoy a family picnic in the fresh air while experiencing

An eagle at Spier Wine Farm

and learning about animals and conservation. Species include giraffe, zebra, eland, bontebok, springbok, impala, teals, love-birds and parrots. ◈ *Map D2 • Cnr R304 (towards Stellenbosch) and R101 (towards Paarl) • 021 884 4506 • Open 9am–5pm daily • Adm • www. giraffehouse.co.za*

Penguins at the Two Oceans Aquarium

Spier Wine Farm
The most child-friendly of the Cape wine estates, Spier has a number of playgrounds and an exciting eagle encounter programme with shows as well as the chance for encounters with Wahlberg's eagles and black eagles *(see p83)*.

Ratanga Junction
This vast theme park to the north of the city has rides for the entire family, including an 18-m (59-ft) water ride (Monkey Falls) and the Cobra roller coaster. Options such as dodgem cars and a mini-Ferris are more child-oriented. There is also a nine-hole putt-putt course, Slingshot and a petting zoo in summer. ◈ *Map B2 • Century Blvd, Century City • 021 550 8504 • Open 10am–5pm daily (only for the Western Cape school holidays) • Adm for rides • www.ratanga.co.za*

Drakenstein Lion Park
The best place to see lions in the Cape Town area is this park near Paarl, which provides sanctuary to captive-born lions that cannot be introduced into the wild. Viewing plat-forms overlook large enclosures that house the 35 lions. Include a trip to nearby Butterfly World when you visit *(see p84)*.

Two Oceans Aquarium
South Africa's leading aquarium boasts an extraordinary diversity of marine life, both from the chilly Atlantic and the warmer Indian Ocean on the east coast. The penguins, sharks and giant rays are a favourite with children. A free activity centre hosts puppet shows and a variety of arts and crafts. Visit at feeding time *(see p10)*.

Imhoff Farm
This restored 18th-century farm en route to Cape Point is a delight for kids, with domestic animals roaming freely in the Higgeldy Piggeldy Farmyard. There is also a snake park. Activities for kids include pony and camel rides. A pleasant coffee shop sells hand-made cheese. ◈ *Map G4 • Kommetjie • 021 783 4545 • Open 10am–5pm Tue–Sun • www.imhofffarm.co.za*

Feeding time for lions in the Drakenstein Lion Park is at 4pm on Mon, Wed and Fri.

Left **Kirstenbosch National Botanical Garden** Right **Mountain biking, De Hoop Nature Reserve**

TOP 10 Parks and Reserves

1 Table Mountain National Park

Proclaimed as a national park in 1998, this urban park extends from Signal Hill in the north to Cape Point at the tip of the Cape Peninsula. This rich biodiversity, with an estimated 2,000 plant species and fauna from Chacma baboons to endemic birds and frogs, thrives within metropolitan Cape Town. ✆ *Map T4 • 021 712 2337 • Opening hrs vary for each section • Adm for select sections • www.sanparks.org*

2 Kirstenbosch National Botanical Garden

On the eastern slopes of Table Mountain, these landscaped gardens show-case South Africa's huge variety of flora, and can be explored on a network of well-maintained, mostly wheelchair-friendly footpaths *(see pp20–21)*.

3 Silvermine Nature Reserve

Part of the central section of Table Mountain National Park, Silvermine is a lovely, refreshing alternative to the Table Mountain massif. The Silvermine River Walk provides an introduction to *fynbos* vegetation and birdlife, while the steeper walk to Noordhoek Peak and Elephant's Eye Cave offers spectacular oceanic views. ✆ *Map B4 • 021 789 2457 • Open May–Sep 8am–5pm; Oct–Apr 7am–6pm • Adm • www.sanparks.org/parks/table_mountain*

4 De Hoop Nature Reserve

This reserve supports plant, bird and mammal species in the world's largest surviving tract of coastal *fynbos*. It stretches inland to the craggy Potberg, a breeding site for the endangered **Cape Cormorant** Cape vulture. Used mostly by hikers and cyclists, it can also be explored by road *(see p95)*.

5 Jonkershoek and Assegaaibosch Nature Reserves

A ramblers' paradise, these adjoining reserves protect the Jonkershoek Mountains, which rise 1,526 m (5,005 ft) on the eastern outskirts of Stellenbosch. Apart from the wildlife and montane *fynbos*, it also offers day walks, ranging from a stroll through the Assegaaibosch wild-flower garden, to the challenging 18-km (9-mile) Swartbroskloof Trail *(see p83)*.

Watsonia flowers in spring at Jonkershoek Nature Reserve

6 Table Bay Nature Reserve

Located in suburban Milnerton and Table View, this reserve is one of the top bird-watching sites in Cape Town and provides protection to the Diep River floodplain, which attracts freshwater and marine birds. Almost

Harold Porter National Botanical Garden

200 species have been recorded to date. Between October and March, there is an influx of migrant waders. There are two hides and a footpath here. ⊗ Map B2 • Grey Ave, Table View • 021 557 5509 • Open 7:30am–5:30pm daily • Adm • www.friendsofrietvlei.co.za

7 Harold Porter National Botanical Garden

This botanical garden in Betty's Bay is an excellent place to get familiar with *fynbos* flora, including the *Disa uniflora* in its natural habitat, proteas, ericas and restios. The birdlife found in the garden is an added attraction for avid birdwatchers, with most *fynbos* endemics well-represented (see p98).

8 Paarl Mountain Nature Reserve

Situated on the outskirts of Paarl, with a mix of montane *fynbos* and indigenous forests, this reserve protects the granite domes, which give the town its name. Good for a bracing walk, the spot is frequented by anglers and mountain bikers. ⊗ Map E1 • Jan Phillips Mountain Dr, Paarl • 021 807 4500 • Open summer 7am–7pm daily; winter 7am–6pm daily • Adm, fee for use of a vehicle

9 West Coast National Park

Centred on the sheltered Langebaan Lagoon, this sprawling marine park is popular with bird and watersport enthusiasts. Apart from the coastal scenery, attractions include wildlife such as eland, bontebok and springbok. Visit in August–September, when the blooming wildflowers in the Postberg section are a stunning sight (see p96).

10 Bird Island Nature Reserve

This rocky outcrop, lying offshore of the west coast port of Lamberts Bay, is the world's only accessible breeding colony of the striking Cape gannet birds. The island also hosts Cape cormorants, penguins and seals. ⊗ Map S1 • Lamberts Bay • 0861 227 362 8873 • Open 7am–6pm daily, summer 7am–7pm daily • Adm • www.capenature.co.za

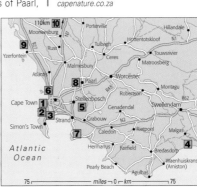

Left **Seals sunning themselves at Seal Island, Hout Bay** Right **Harbour cruise**

🔟 Wildlife Experiences

1 Birdwatching at Rondevlei Nature Reserve

This large wetland on the Cape Flats is easily the best place to spot waterbirds in suburban Cape Town. Among the 230 species recorded are the great white pelican, African spoonbill and various herons. Look out for their ever-present but shy family of hippos. Ⓢ *Map I3* • *Perth Rd, Rondevlei* • *021 706 2404* • *Open 7:30am–5pm, closes 7pm Sat & Sun from Dec–Feb* • *Adm* • *www.rondevlei.co.za; www.capetown.gov. za/en/environmentalresourcemanagement*

2 Harbour Cruise

Operators on the V&A Waterfront offer cruises through Table Bay, with a near certainty of sighting Cape fur seals and various gulls and terns. On a good day you might also catch sight of dolphins *(see pp10–11)*.

3 Dassies on Table Mountain

Watch the endearing semi-tame dassies (hyraxes) sunbathing on Table Mountain. Resembling guinea pigs, but larger and sharper-toothed, these oddball creatures are dwarfish relics of a group of ungulates that dominated the African herbivore niche about 35 million years ago *(see pp18–19)*.

4 Penguin Colony, Boulders Beach

Waddling around like tipsy tuxedoed waiters, these flightless birds are a firm fixture on the tourist itinerary. Amazingly, the 2,000-strong Boulder colony was founded by two breeding pairs in 1982 *(see pp24–5)*.

5 Seal Island, Near Hout Bay

A flat granite outcrop 6 km (4 miles) offshore, this island supports the Western Cape's largest seal colony (up to 73,000 individuals), along with some penguins and three species of cormorant. Though visitors are not allowed to mingle with the animals, boat tours run past the seal-lined shores *(see p79)*.

6 Cape of Good Hope

The most southerly sector of Table Mountain National Park, the Cape of Good Hope boasts spectacular oceanic viewpoints. It also offers excellent wildlife watching – localized endemics such as bontebok, grysbok and mountain zebra coexist with the chacma baboon, eland and small grey mongoose *(see pp26–7)*.

African penguin on Boulders Beach

Caged shark dives

Land-Based Whale Watching

The Western Cape has the world's best land-based whale watching. Cliffs at Hermanus, De Hoop and False Bay offer vantage points to view the southern right whale breaching in the deep, sheltered bays. ◈ *Peak season Jun–Nov; calving season Jul–Aug*

Caged Shark Dives

Caged dives to see the great white shark in rapacious action rank as the ultimate submarine wildlife encounter for thrill-seekers. At the ever-popular Gansbaai, 160 km (99.5 miles) from Cape Town; the number of passengers is limited, so each diver is able to have more close encounters. ◈ *Shark Cage Diving: 021 671 4777 • www.sharkcagediving.co.za*

Scuba Diving and Snorkelling

The kelp forests and deep tidal pools of the Atlantic offer some excellent opportunities for diving into the deep to glimpse weird and wonderful marine creatures.

Inverdoorn Game Reserve

A spectacular reserve in the immensity of the Karoo and only a few hours' drive from Cape Town. It is rich in wildlife, including lions, cheetahs, giraffe, antelope and white rhino. A range of leisure activities are also available. ◈ *Map U4 • off R46 • 021 434 4639 • www.inverdoorn.com*

Top 10 Endemic Flora and Fauna

King Protea
This pineapple-sized salmon-pink bloom is South Africa's national flower.

Red Disa
The "Pride of Table Mountain", this pretty red flower blooms Dec–Jan.

Silver Tree
Restricted to the Cape Peninsula, this odd protea-affiliated tree has silver-haired stems and cone-like flowers.

African Penguin
The only penguin that breeds in South Africa. Two other sub-Antarctic species turn up occasionally on the Cape's beaches.

Bontebok
This beautifully marked antelope was on the verge of extinction in the 20th century.

Cape Dwarf Chameleon
The most readily observed of four chameleon species from the Western Cape mountains.

Cape Mountain Zebra
Rescued from extinction, the Cape Mountain Zebra has fared better than its close relative, the quagga, hunted out in the 19th century.

Cape Sugarbird
This long-tailed *fynbos* dweller belongs to a family whose range is limited to South Africa and Zimbabwe.

Orange-Breasted Sunbird
Dazzling nectar-eater limited to flowering *fynbos* habitats.

Table Mountain Ghost Frog
Seldom seen, this club-fingered frog is known from just the seven specific streams on Table Mountain.

Fynbos is a type of heath-like scrub cover confined to the Cape coast of South Africa.

Left **Beach huts at Muizenberg** Right **The shores of Boulders Beach**

⌐10 Beaches

1 Clifton Beach
Situated within easy walking distance of Sea Point and Green Point, perennially fashionable Clifton is the closest swimming beach to the city centre. Of the four sandy coves divided by granite outcrops, Fourth Beach has the best facilities, including changing rooms, public toilets, snack and soda kiosks. Deck chairs and umbrellas are available for daily rental. The waters are relatively chilly and the undertow should not be underestimated (see p62).

2 Camps Bay
Overlooked by the spectacular Twelve Apostles formation on the western face of Table Mountain, this wide, sandy beach lies alongside the main road through Camps Bay below a row of trendy street cafés, restaurants and bars. A popular haunt with families over the holidays, it is generally quieter at other times. Deck chairs and umbrellas are available for hire at this beach (see p61).

3 Sandy Bay
Protected by high dunes and dotted with secluded rocky coves for sunbathing, Sandy Bay near Llandudno has long been a semi-official nudist beach. It also hosts something of a gay scene, though by no means exclusively so. It is relatively inaccessible by public transport, and often too chilly for swimming. ◈ Map G2

4 Noordhoek
Set below spectacular Chapman's Peak (see p61), Noordhoek is a seemingly endless arc of glorious white sand near Kommetjie. Though too exposed to the elements to host much of a beach scene, it attracts walkers, birdwatchers and horse riders. Perfect for a long seaside stroll (see p78).

5 Muizenberg
Along the northern shore of False Bay, Muizenberg was Cape Town's trendiest beach in the 1960s, but its glitz has now faded. Still, it is usually safe for swimming and excellent for surfing. The varied facilities, including a protected pool, water-slides, miniature golf course, snack shops and colourful changing rooms, ensure that the beach remains a favourite with families. It is very accessible by train from the city centre (see p77).

Camps Bay with Lion's Head in the background

The rocky shores of Seaforth Beach

Cape of Good Hope

Set below Cape Point, this windswept beach is arguably the most beautiful on the peninsula. As well as attracting sunbathers and swimmers, the Cape is also a magnet for walkers and nature enthusiasts *(see pp26–7)*.

Boulders Beach

This is a lovely, secluded beach on the southern fringe of the penguin colony *(see p42)*. Enjoy the company of these remarkable birds, who bustle fearlessly around the same rocks where tourists sunbathe. An entrance fee is required *(see p25)*.

Seaforth Beach

Like nearby Boulders, this beach, within walking distance of Simon's Town, is hemmed in by gigantic rocks. Generally, it is not too busy, and there's a chance of spotting stray penguins waddling past. The charming Seaforth Restaurant with its wooden balcony overlooks the beach *(see p25)*.

Bikini Beach, Strand

Less than an hour's drive east of Cape Town, secluded Bikini Beach is the most popular of the many beaches around Strand. Overlooked by the Helderberg Mountains, it offers clear views across False Bay. The shallow waters are safe for swimming, and an abundance of cafés and restaurants make it very popular with families. If the sunbathing gets monotonous, there are some great tidal rock pools at nearby Gordon's Bay. ◈ *Map D4*

Bloubergstrand

The *blouberg* (blue mountain) referred to is Table Mountain *(see pp18–19)*, whose flat-topped profile is displayed in full glory on a clear day. Sandy for the most part, Bloubergstrand has enough rocky protrusions to keep it interesting. Though rather exposed in windy weather, the beach is a favourite with water-sport enthusiasts *(see p61)*.

Left **Golf course in Steenberg** Centre **Chiefs and Stormers rugby match** Right **Horseback riding**

🔟 Sports and Outdoor Activities

Rugby
Traditionally one of the world's top sides, the South African "Springboks" have twice won the Rugby World Cup (in 1995 and 2007). International matches are held at Newlands, the home stadium of Western Province, Cape Town's provincial and Super Rugby side.

Football
Athlone Stadium on the Cape Flats is home to the Premier League Team Ajax Cape Town. Cape Town Stadium in Green Point was rebuilt for the 2010 FIFA World Cup in South Africa. ◈ *Athlone Stadium: Map J1; 021 637 6607 • Cape Town Stadium: Map N1; 021 417 0101*

Cricket
The Newlands Cricket Stadium is home to the Western Cape provincial side, which has produced several international players. At least one five-day test match and many One Day Internationals are played here every year. ◈ *Newlands Stadium: Map J2: 021 657 2003*

Deep-Sea and Fly-Fishing
The waters off the Cape Peninsula are renowned for their great deep-sea fishing, with tuna being a speciality.

The mountain streams inland offer great fly-fishing opportunities. ◈ *Fly-fishing: Inkwazi: 083 626 0467, www.inkwaziflyfishing.co.za; deep-sea trips: Big Blue Fishing Charters: 083 777 1048*

Golfing
There are several golf courses in the Cape Town area. Two of the best are Rondebosch Golf Course and the Atlantic Beach Golf Estate. ◈ *Rondebosch Golf Course: Map B3; 021 689 4176, Atlantic Beach: Map B2; 021 553 2223*

Horse Riding, Noordhoek
The sandy Noordhoek Beach below Chapman's Peak is great for horse riding. Lessons are available for all ages, as well as disabled riders. ◈ *Sleepy Hollow: 021 789 2341; www.sleepyhollowhorseriding.co.za*

Mountain Biking
The mountainous winelands offer endless opportunities for keen cyclists and several

Surfing at a reef, Dungeon, off Cape Town

Details of all golf courses are available on www.sa-venues.com/ golf_courses_south_africa.htm.

Hikers atop Table Mountain

reserves have mountain-bike trails. Bikes can be hired in all the main centres, but the best agent for specialist riding trips is Downhill Adventures. ✪ *Downhill Adventures: 021 422 0388, www. downhilladventures.com*

Hiking in the Cape Fold Mountains

Hiking trails suitable for all levels of fitness traverse most of the nature reserves and national parks, offering an opportunity to explore the wildlife. Most can be walked unguided, but it's best to take along an experienced guide. ✪ *Cape Eco-Tours: 021 919 2282, www. cape-ecotours.co.za*

Surfing

The Western Cape offers some of the world's best surfing. The part of False Bay around Muizenberg is usually reliable, but busy in summer. Sites along the Atlantic seaboard are less busy and more challenging.

Kayaking and Canoeing in False Bay

Starting from Simon's Town, ideally on a windless day, paddle through scenic False Bay, and look for penguins, dolphins and whales. Experienced adrenaline junkies prefer to kayak in stormy weather.

Top 10 South African Sporting Icons

1 Ernie Els
The former world number-one golfer, known as the Big Easy, has won four major titles.

2 Makhaya Ntini
South Africa's first black international cricketer reached number 2 in world rankings for Test bowlers in 2006.

3 Benni McCarthy
His 31 international goals are a South African record he shares with fellow Capetonian footballer Shaun Bartlett.

4 Francois Pienaar
He captained the South African rugby team, which won the 1995 Rugby World Cup on their home turf.

5 Shaun Pollock
This former national cricket captain is a top-ranked bowling all-rounder (416 wickets/3,781 runs in Tests).

6 Chad le Clos
This swimmer beat Michael Phelps for gold in the 200-m butterfly at the 2012 London Olympics.

7 Penny Heyns
An Olympic gold medallist who won the 100-m and 200-m breaststroke in 1996 – the first ever woman to achieve this amazing feat.

8 Roland Schoeman
Holder of three swimming world records and a member of the triumphant relay team at the 2004 Olympics.

9 Lucas Radebe
Former South Africa and Leeds captain, he played in the football team that won the 1996 Africa Nations Cup.

10 John Smit
Captain of the Springbok rugby team that won the 2007 Rugby World Cup.

Left **Tourists exploring a cave** Right **Rock climbers at Table Mountain**

📷10 Adventure Activities

1 Paragliding
A spectacular location for paragliding, Cape Town and the surrounding winelands are best explored with a guide at first. Birdmen Paragliding offers day trips with radio contact, longer excursions from three days to a month, and introductory and full-licence courses. ✆ *Birdmen Paragliding: 082 658 6710; www.birdmen.co.za*

2 Winelands Ballooning
A blissful way to start the day is to glide serenely over the beautiful winelands around Paarl in a hot-air balloon. Leave at sunrise, letting the wind navigate the balloon until you land, from where a support vehicle takes you for a champagne breakfast. ✆ *021 863 3192; runs Nov–May only, weather permitting; www.kapinfo.com*

3 Helicopter Rides
There is no more thrilling a way of seeing the Cape Peninsula and Table Mountain than from the air, when weather permits. You can charter a helicopter from the V&A Waterfront. ✆ *Base 4: 021 934 4405; www.base4.co.za*

4 Caving
The network of sandstone caverns above Kalk Bay is reached via a rather steep footpath offering stunning views over False Bay. The earliest evidence of human habitation at the Cape was excavated within these caves. It requires a bit of clambering and crawling to explore the cavernous depths properly. Be sure to carry a torch. ✆ *Zafari Travel: 082 979 2632; www.zafaritravel.co.za*

5 Scuba Diving
The coast to the north of Durban is renowned for its offshore reefs teeming with colourful fish. However, the chillier waters off Cape Town also provide great diving possibilities – immense forests of swaying kelp, friendly seals on the Atlantic seaboard, and a large number of shipwrecks everywhere. ✆ *Scuba Shack: 072 603 8630; www.scubashack.co.za*

6 Quad Biking
The natural beauty in and around Cape Town makes it a great place for quad biking. Experienced guides will show you how to operate the bike

Paraglider launching off Lion's Head Mountain

Abseiling along the western face of Table Mountain

before taking you on an exciting ride through the many tracks and trails across Cape Peninsula and the Winelands. ⬡ *Downhill Adventures: 021 422 0388; www. downhilladventures.com*

River Rafting

The closest site for river rafting is the Breede River, which runs through the Robertson Valley lying to the northeast of Cape Town. Umkulu Safaris arrange day and overnight trips. They also run ambitious four- and six-day rafting trips on the Orange River along the border with Namibia. ⬡ *Umkulu Trails: 021 853 7952; www.umkulu.co.za*

Kloofing

One of the most popular activities out of Cape Town is to go *kloofing* – jumping into freshwater pools from cliffs up to 15 m (49 ft) high – in the Boland Mountains north of Cape Town. The best sites, including the ominously named Suicide Gorge, are reached after a fairly long hike. Not an activity for the unfit or the faint of heart! ⬡ *Absolute Adventures: 021 531 6616; www.absoluteadventures.co.za*

Abseiling

For spectacular heart-stopping views from Table Mountain, take in Abseil Africa's 112-m (367-ft) controlled descent of the western face. It is considered the world's original highest commercial abseil. ⬡ *Abseil Africa: 021 424 4760; www.abseilafrica.co.za*

Rock Climbing

The craggy Western Cape peaks are a rock climber's paradise. City Rock is the leading centre to visit for a good selection of climbing gear or experienced instructors. It also has an indoor climbing centre. ⬡ *City Rock: 021 447 1326; call ahead to book a course; www.cityrock.co.za*

Kloofing, or jumping, into freshwater pools

Abseiling is the process of descending from a fixed rope; the American term for it is rappelling.

Left **Bo-Kaap Museum** Right **Art depictions at the Red Shed Workshop**

Exploring Local Culture

District Six Museum

This emotionally charged museum is a testament to the iniquitous Group Areas Act passed by the National Party in the 1950s–60s. The museum focuses on day-to-day life in District Six before apartheid's bulldozers rumbled in *(see pp14–15)*.

Slave Lodge

This double-storey building opposite the Company's Garden was founded in 1679 as basic quarters for the wretched immigrants – the force behind the Cape's agricultural economy – who were imported from Malaysia and Indian Ocean islands. Now a museum, it charts the local and international history of the slave trade through a series of multimedia displays *(see pp8–9)*.

Display at Bo-Kaap Museum

Rock Art Gallery, South African Museum

South Africa is one of the world's most important repositories of rock art, with several sites dating back 10,000 years scattered through the country. The Rock Art Gallery has a superb display on this powerful prehistoric medium, including re-creations and an original panel relocated here to prevent damage by roadworks. ® *Map P5* • *25 Queen Victoria St* • *021 481 3800* • *Open 10am–5pm daily* • *Adm* • *www.iziko.org.za*

Langa

Founded in 1927, the oldest black township in Cape Town is also closest to the city centre. It was integral to the resistance to apartheid. Tours to Langa include the Tsoga Environmental Resource Centre and Gugu S'Thebe Arts Centre *(see p74)*.

Long Street

Affordable restaurants, quirky shops, tour operators and a smattering of gay-friendly nightspots line Long Street, one of the liveliest and most integrated parts of the city. Sleazy and trendy in equal parts, it is the hub of the city's backpacker scene *(see p63)*.

Red Shed Craft Workshop

This cavernous workshop has potters, candlemakers and other artisans at work. You can buy individualized handmade souvenirs or, with enough notice, have special orders fulfilled. ® *Map Q1* • *The V&A Waterfront* • *www.waterfront.co.za*

Residents of Langa

Imizamo Yethu township

7 Meeting a Former Inmate at Robben Island

A trip to Robben Island ends with a tour of the high-security prison where anti-apartheid activists were incarcerated. With a former prisoner as your guide, get a first-hand account of time spent in South Africa's oldest political prison *(see pp12–13)*.

8 Khayelitsha

An isiXhosa phrase meaning "Our New Home", Khayelitsha, on the Cape Flats, started life in the 1950s after the Group Areas Act was passed. Recognized as a township only in 1985, it is one of South Africa's poorest urban centres *(see p74)*.

9 Bo-Kaap Museum

This museum explores the evolution of the Bo-Kaap *(see p62)* – an Islamic suburb inhabited by the Cape Malay people since the abolition of slavery in the 1830s. ◉ *Map Q4 • 71 Wale St, Bo-Kaap • 021 481 3938 • Open 10am–5pm Mon–Sat • Adm • www.iziko.org.za*

10 Imizamo Yethu

A recent township, Imizamo Yethu is situated on the slopes above Hout Bay. The welcoming atmosphere makes up for the primitive conditions. Do not miss the tours provided by the residents *(see p78)*.

Top 10 Slang Words and Phrases

1 Ag!

Pronounced like the Scots "Och", this can be an expression of distaste (Ag, sis!), sympathy (Ag, shame!) or annoyance (Ag, no!).

2 Bru

Derived from the Afrikaans *broer* (brother), this is a generic term of male address, a bit like "dude" in the USA or "mate" in the UK.

3 Dop

An alcoholic beverage – or the act of drinking one (as in "let's have a quick dop").

4 Babalas

A colourful Cape Coloured term for a hangover.

5 Ek sé

Literally "I say", the phrase is used to prefix a statement or request in the same way.

6 Izzit?

Literally "Is it", this phrase is often interjected when another person speaks. It is similar to the English "really?"

7 Moerse

Very – as in "it's moerse cold" on a cold day. Used to emphasize something.

8 Lekker

Good or nice (as in "we had a lekker time"). It can also mean tasty. Sweets (candies) are called *lekkers* in Afrikaans.

9 Just Now

This misleading phrase, which frequently confuses and amuses visitors to Cape Town, means "a bit later" – or "much later"!

10 Jol

The word means party or any good time, and is used both as a noun ("where's the jol?") or a verb ("let's jol").

Left **Belthazar Restaurant & Wine Bar** Right **La Colombe**

Wining and Dining

1 Belthazar Restaurant & Wine Bar

Former winner of the Best Steakhouse in South Africa, this popular restaurant on the V&A Waterfront is the place to go for a prime fillet or rump. More than 100 of the Cape's finest wines are available by the glass, while sought-after rare vintages are available by the bottle (see p68).

2 Den Anker Restaurant and Bar

Set on a small jetty, this is one of the Waterfront's top eateries. It serves Belgian specialities, such as rabbit, fine wines and good Belgian beers. Eat outdoors with a view of seals and boats in the harbour. In poor weather, the boat-shaped bar compensates for being indoors (see p68).

3 Africa Café

This eatery, renowned for its evening buffet of pan-African dishes, provides a "flying tour" of Africa's varied flavours. The lively bar is reason enough to linger after the buffet (see p69).

Den Anker Restaurant and Bar

4 Savoy Cabbage

This is one of Cape Town's trendiest eateries, set in a restored Victorian building in the city centre. The historic setting is offset by a funky interior, and the imaginative menu is strong on game, shellfish and vegetarian dishes (see p69).

5 La Colombe

Set among Constantia's vineyards, this restaurant is consistently rated as one of Cape Town's best. High quality local ingredients are given a saucy French touch, plus a dash of Asian fusion. The irresistible menu is informally placed on a chalkboard and the food is enjoyed in a courtyard (see p75).

6 Jordan Restaurant

Contemporary dishes feature local meats and seafood such as springbok and West Coast mussels. Renowned chef George Jardine changes the menu daily to make use of seasonal fare. Floor-to-ceiling windows maximise the stunning views of the dam, surrounding vineyards and mountains (see p90).

7 The Foodbarn

Many of Cape Town's best chefs cite Franck Dangereux – owner/chef of The Foodbarn – as their mentor, after his previous work at La Colombe. Expect superb French-influenced food, sublime sauces and boutique wines by the carafe, in the

Jordan Restaurant

laid-back and peaceful village of Noordhoek, on the South Peninsula *(see p81)*.

Terroir
Classic pairings can make dishes appear deceptively simple, but the chef knows how to increase the flavours without overpowering the natural attributes of the seasonal produce. Take your cue from the slow cooking methods and make it a long dining experience, accompanied by estate wines *(see p90)*.

Le Quartier Français
The ultimate culinary splash-out is the Tasting Room at Le Quartier Français in central Franschhoek. Among the world's finest restaurants, it serves an eclectic selection of food and is anything but cheap. The stylish iCi Restaurant in the same building offers an affordable opportunity to sample the Le Quartier style *(see p91)*.

Le Pique-Nique
Something about the Winelands invites lingering lawn picnics with chilled white wine. No estate offers this facility with as much panache as the Boschendal estate and its moderately pretentious Le Pique-Nique, set below shady pines and blue mountains *(see p91)*.

Top 10 South African Dishes and Delicacies

Bobotie
A Cape Malay classic of minced beef and yellow rice, sweetened by raisins, and topped with an egg sauce.

Potjiekos
Meat and vegetable stew cooked slowly in a *potjie* (a small black pot) over an open fire.

Waterblommetjie Bredie
A Cape stew made of lamb and *waterblommetjie*, a water plant which resembles an artichoke.

Tomato Bredie
A thick, tasty tomato-based stew made of succulent Karoo lamb.

Boerewors
Spicy, fatty "Farmer's sausage", best *braaied* (barbecued) on an open fire.

Malva Pudding
This sweet, spongy Dutch pudding is made with apricots.

Melktert
This dish is a milkier and sweeter version of a custard tart. Dates back to Cape Malay-Dutch cooking.

Koeksister
Translated as "Cake sisters", this is a spiral pastry with a doughnut-like texture and a sticky-sweet coating.

Pap 'n' Stew
The traditional staple in most of South Africa, this is a meat stew that is eaten along with *mealie pap* (maize porridge).

Biltong
Spicy strips of dried, salted and spiced raw beef or game meat, biltong is reminiscent of beef jerky.

 For more restaurants and their price categories, **see pp68, 75, 81, 90–91 and 99.**

Ladysmith Black Mambazo performing at the Cape Town International Jazz Festival

🔟 Festivals and Events

1 Kaapse Klopse
Also known as the Cape Minstrel Festival, this colourful New Year's welcome originated as a response by former slaves to a 1848 visit by "blackfaces" (white American minstrels who blackened their faces with burnt cork). Local people paint their faces white and march through Cape Town. 🖎 *2 Jan*

2 Maynardville Open-Air Theatre
The 720-seat open-air theatre in Maynardville Park has hosted a Shakespeare-in-the-Park Festival since 1956, when *The Taming of the Shrew* was first performed here. It attracts up to 20,000 patrons annually. 🖎 *Map I2 • Cnr of Church and Wolf Sts, Wynberg • 021 421 7695 • Jan–Feb • www.maynardville.co.za*

3 Cape Town Pride Festival
The city's most important gay festival was inaugurated in 2001. Pride Parade Day attracts a stream of colourful floats and involves drag shows, fashion events and an after party. Other events in the flamboyant fortnight-long festival include pageants, balls, tea parties and gay movies. 🖎 *info@capetownpride.org • Feb–March • www.capetownpride.org*

4 Cape Town Festival
Cape Town's most important arts festival began in 1999 to promote integration and celebrate the multi-racial communities of Cape Town.

It is held in March or April in The Company's Garden *(see pp8–9)*. 🖎 *021 465 9042 • Apr • www.capetownfestival.co.za*

5 Cape Town International Jazz Festival
South Africa's premier jazz event. Performers have included Gino Vannelli, Randy Crawford, Ladysmith Black Mambazo and Themba Mkhize. 🖎 *021 671 8716 • Mar last weekend • www.capetownjazzfest.com*

6 Stellenbosch Wine Festival
Wine-lovers descend on Stellenbosch for this week-long event that features more than 500 wines by over 100 Cape estates. The festival includes wine-tasting tutorials, craft workshops and kids' entertainment. 🖎 *Map D2 • 021 886 4310 • Jan/Feb • www.wineroute.co.za*

7 Hermanus Whale Festival
Late September is when Hermanus holds its annual whale festival. This week-long programme at Market Square

Kaapse Klopse

Eggman at the Hermanus Whale Festival

involves live music concerts, sporting events and sightings of the world's largest living creatures. ◈ *Map U5* • *028 313 0928* • *Oct* • *www.whalefestival.co.za*

Cape Town Comedy Festival

Inaugurated in 1997, this annual comedy festival featuring local and international comedians is held at the Cape Town International Convention Centre. ◈ *info@huntalive.com* • *Book on www. computicket.com or call 0861 915 8000* • *Sep* • *www.comedyfestival.co.za*

Kirstenbosch Summer Sunset Concerts

A wonderful way to enjoy a Sunday sunset. The open-air concerts on the lawns appeal to all musical tastes and are performed within the beautiful botanic gardens. ◈ *Map H2* • *Rhodes Avenue, Newlands* • *021 799 8783*

Oude Libertas Summer Festival

This music festival at the historic Oude Libertas Estate on the Papegaaiberg has an eclectic programme, from chamber music to jazz and *boeremusiek* (Afrikaans folk). ◈ *Stellenbosch* • *021 809 7000* • *Dec–Mar* • *www. oudelibertas.co.za*

Top 10 Local Things to Buy

1 Scarab Paper
Write on handmade writing paper produced from elephant dung using an ancient Chinese technique.

2 Ndebele Beadwork
A wide range of kaleidoscopic necklaces, bracelets and anklets from the Limpopo Province.

3 Zulu Basketry
The Zulu, South Africa's most populous ethnic group, are skilled weavers.

4 Swazi Candles
Multicoloured and interestingly shaped candles are produced in Swaziland and Mpumalanga.

5 Amarula
This creamy liqueur is produced from the endemic apricot-like marula fruit.

6 Music CDs
Any decent CD shop will stock a good selection of introductory CDs to the bustling local music scene.

7 Ostrich Leatherware
High-quality handbags are crafted from the hide of the world's largest bird.

8 Mohair Scarves and Shawls
Own an article that is made from what is reputed to be the world's finest and softest mohair.

9 Wine
Serious connoisseurs of wine can save a fortune by buying locally. Make arrangements in order to specially ship bottles home.

10 African Fine Arts
Many shops sell fine African masks, carvings and batiks, mostly from north of the Limpopo.

AROUND TOWN

CAPE TOWN & THE WINELANDS' TOP 10

Left **Main entrance, Castle of Good Hope** Right **A path through the Company's Garden**

Central Cape Town

THE HISTORIC HEART OF SOUTH AFRICA'S *oldest city is bound by Table Bay to the north and Table Mountain to the south. Signal Hill forms an imposing barrier between the City Bowl's inner city suburbs and those along the Atlantic seaboard. The large number of historic buildings, excellent museums, cinemas, restaurants and nightclubs, together with a buzzing street life, confirm the city's status as one of Africa's major cultural centres. But the*

undoubted highlight, whether you are standing on the Castle of Good Hope's ramparts or nursing a chilled beer at a waterfront café, is Table Mountain, looming over the city centre with effortless majesty.

The façade of the evocative District Six Museum

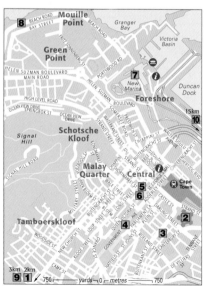

🔟 Sights

1. Table Mountain
2. Castle of Good Hope
3. District Six Museum
4. The Company's Garden
5. Greenmarket Square
6. Michaelis Collection
7. The V&A Waterfront
8. Beach Road
9. Camps Bay
10. Bloubergstrand

Left sidebar: Around Town – Central Cape Town

Preceding pages **The shores of Boulders Beach, Simon's Town**

Table Mountain

The 1,067-m (3,500-ft) high plateau of Table Mountain is reached by a rotating cablecar that offers 360° views across the city centre to the distant Hottentots Holland Mountains. At the top, a network of footpaths allows you to explore the *fynbos* vegetation and assorted wildlife. Maclear's Beacon, the highest summit, is less than an hour from the upper cableway. The adventurous traveller might like to undertake Abseil Africa's controlled 112-m (367-ft) descent from a ledge overlooking Camps Bay *(see pp18–19)*.

Castle of Good Hope

Constructed in 1666–79, Cape Town's oldest building (and a superbly preserved example of a Dutch East India Company fort) now stands inland as a result of land reclamation. An imposing slate and sandstone pentagon, the rather utilitarian design is alleviated by the sculpted masonry on the bell tower and the Anton Anreith bas-relief above the Kat Balcony. An interesting military museum and the 19th-century William Fehr collection of art are also housed here *(see pp16–17)*.

District Six Museum

This moving tribute to District Six, bulldozed in the apartheid era *(see p34)*, is housed in the former Buitenkant Methodist Church, whose association with the anti-apartheid movement led to its forced closure in 1988. The museum's centrepiece is a vast, annotated floor map of the suburb in its multi-racial heyday. Other exhibits bear witness to the cruelty and destructiveness of the racism that dominated South African life for almost half a century *(see pp14–15)*.

The Company's Garden

Established in 1652 as a vegetable garden to provide fresh produce to Dutch East India Company (VOC) ships docking at Table Bay, the Company's Garden doubles as a botanical garden. At the heart of the so-called Museum Mile, this inner-city park, with a backdrop of Table Mountain, is a lovely spot for relaxing and strolling. You can spend a day exploring the buildings fronting its lawns, such as the Iziko Slave Lodge and the Iziko South African Museum and Planetarium *(see pp8–9)*.

Table Mountain cableway

Michaelis Collection

Greenmarket Square

This cobbled square in the heart of old Cape Town served as a slave market under the Dutch East India Company (VOC) *(see p34)*. Its name, however, alludes to a subsequent incarnation as a fruit and vegetable market that made way for a parking lot in the 1950s. Surrounded by historic buildings, many housing smart eateries and cafés, this graceful square is home to a popular pan-African craft market and an assortment of lively street performers juggling, dancing, singing or performing mimes.
🞄 *Map Q4*

Michaelis Collection

This world-renowned collection of paintings by Dutch and Flemish masters of the Golden Age (16th–18th centuries) was donated to the city by Sir Max Michaelis in 1914. Housed in the beautifully restored Old Townhouse, which

The Khoisan

When Van Riebeeck established Cape Town in 1652 *(see p35)*, the Western Cape had been inhabited by the Khoisan-speaking populace for several millennia. Within 200 years they were gone; some had fallen victim to diseases while others were killed by gun-toting settlers. Those who remained integrated into the mixed-race community, Cape Coloureds.

served as the City Hall until 1905, the structure is counted among the foremost architectural gems of the city. It exemplifies the early Cape Rococo style with its graceful triple-arched portico and pretty belfry. 🞄 *Map P4*
• *Greenmarket Square* • *021 481 3970*
• *Open 10am–5pm Mon–Sat* • *Adm R20*
• *www.iziko.org.za*

The V&A Waterfront

Cape Town's reconstituted harbour is also the city's foremost shopping venue. Literally hundreds of shops, ranging from bland chain stores to quirky craft stalls, can be found alongside several restaurants and a host of tourist spots, including the Nelson Mandela Gateway. Boat and helicopter operators offer harbour cruises and flights over Table Mountain *(see pp10–11)*.

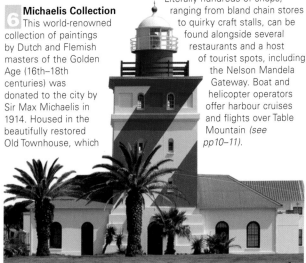

The Green Point Lighthouse, Beach Road

Waterfront buildings, Camps Bay

Beach Road
Passing through the suburbs of Green Point and Sea Point immediately west of the city centre, Beach Road runs along an attractive stretch of Atlantic coastline. The road is separated from the sea by a grassy promenade where locals jog, skateboard and walk their dogs. It's a great spot for some aimless wandering, especially at sunset. Also worth seeing is the Green Point Lighthouse, the oldest in the country. ✎ *Map K3*

Camps Bay
Wonderfully set between mountain and sea, Camps Bay is where suburban Cape Town's Atlantic seaboard gives way to the wild and unspoilt coastal scenery of the Cape Peninsula. This idyllic suburb boasts one of the nicest beaches in greater Cape Town and has a fine range of restaurants and bars situated on its waterfront. ✎ *Map H1*

Bloubergstrand
This long sandy beach 12 km (7 miles) north of the city centre offers the most spectacular view of Cape Town; Table Bay glittering in the foreground against a backdrop of Table Mountain in its flat-topped glory. The beach, though busy with locals in summer, is seldom crowded. There's a fair chance of spotting dolphins and whales in season in the chilly waters off the beach. ✎ *Map B2*

A Day in the City Centre

> **Morning**

🕐 After breakfast, make your way to the **District Six Museum** (see pp14–15) and explore its stirring exhibits. Then walk a couple of blocks back down Buitenkant Road to the **Castle of Good Hope**, (see pp16–17) leaving time to admire the **City Hall** (see p17) where Mandela made his first public address after his release in 1990. At the castle, grab a snack at De Goeweneur Restaurant before joining one of the free guided tours that run daily at 11am. At noon, return to the main gate for the firing of the signal cannon. Either drop in at the castle's two museums or enjoy an early lunch at De Goeweneur. Then join the horse-drawn carriage tour of historic Cape Town that departs at 12:45pm and alight at **The Company's Garden** (see pp8–9).

> **Afternoon**

If you didn't have lunch at the castle, there are plenty of choices here. When the weather's right for eating alfresco, **Garden Tea Room** opposite the aviary, has to be first choice. The atmospheric **Crypt Jazz Restaurant** in the crypt of **St George's Cathedral** (see p8) is good on a gloomy day. Afterwards, take a stroll around the gardens, followed by a visit to one of the museums lining them, such as the **National Museum** and **Slave Lodge** (see p8). If you're feeling peckish, stroll to **Mount Nelson Hotel** (see p112) to sample its legendary tea buffet (2:30–5:30pm) before heading back to your hotel.

Left **Bo-Kaap** Centre **Star machine in the Planetarium** Right **South African Museum**

Best of the Rest

1 Planetarium
The centrally located Planetarium has daily shows introducing the dazzling southern sky – worthwhile for those heading into the Karoo, with its clear and brilliant night sky *(see p8)*.

2 St George's Mall
Running through the heart of the historic city centre, this pedestrian mall is usually abuzz with street musicians and busy market stalls. ◎ *Map Q4–Q5*

3 South African Museum
Mainly featuring natural history displays, the South African Museum also exhibits prehistoric rock art *(see p8)*.

4 South African Jewish Museum
Set in the country's oldest synagogue, this fascinating museum documents the history of South Africa's Jewish community. ◎ *Map P6 • 88 Hatfield St • 021 465 1546 • Open 10am–5pm Sun–Thu, 10am–2pm Fri • Adm • www.sajewishmuseum.co.za*

5 Bo-Kaap
The spiritual home of the Cape Malay community, Bo-Kaap (Upper Cape) is known for its colourfully painted houses. Its history is documented in the small Bo-Kaap museum *(see p51)*. ◎ *Map Q4*

6 Gold of Africa Museum
This museum has the world's most comprehensive collection of artifacts from gold-rich African kingdoms. ◎ *Map P4 • 96 Strand St • 021 405 1540 • Open 9:30am–5pm Mon–Sat • Adm • www.goldofafrica.com*

7 Signal Hill and Lion's Head
The climb or drive up Signal Hill is highly rewarding. Aim to be there at dusk for a view over the glittering city. ◎ *Map M3*

8 Clifton Beach
This is the closest of the four beaches to the city centre. It is popular on weekends and over holidays. ◎ *Map A2*

9 Association for the Visual Arts
Dedicated to the advancement of contemporary South African art, this gallery's exhibitions change every three weeks or so. ◎ *Map P4 • 35 Church St • 021 424 7436 • Open 10am–5pm Mon–Fri, 10am–1pm Sat • www.ava.co.za*

10 Iziko Bertram House Museum
Restored in the early 1980s, this Georgian town house contains ten collections, including porcelain items and Georgian furniture. ◎ *Map P6 • Orange St • 021 481 3972 • Open 10am–5pm Mon–Sat • www.iziko.org.za*

To ensure safety, travel around Signal Hill and Lion's Head in a group.

Left **Ethnic jewellery from Greenmarket Square** Right **Victoria Wharf Mall, the V&A Waterfront**

🔟 Shops, Malls and Markets

1 The V&A Waterfront
The Waterfront combines a wonderful harbourfront setting with a selection of shops and restaurants that is second to none *(see pp10–11)*.

2 Long Street
Those seeking a colourful shopping experience will enjoy Long Street's cult, craft and secondhand shops. ◈ *Map P5*

3 Pan African Market
This is an excellent place to check out crafts from all over Africa. Along with a cheerful café, you'll also find a hairdresser and tailor here. ◈ *Map P4 • 76 Long St • 021 426 4478*

4 Greenmarket Square
Situated off Greenmarket Square, Cape Town's oldest flea market has a definite buzz about it. A variety of African crafts can be found alongside ethnically inspired clothing and jewellery *(see p60)*.

5 Cape Quarter
Cape Quarter has a historic location in the trendy De Waterkant suburb and houses shops specializing in crafts and jewellery. It also has several restaurants and cafés. ◈ *Map P3 • 72 Waterkant St • 021 421 1111 • www.cape quarter.co.za*

6 Gardens Shopping Centre
This is the most popular shopping mall in the City Bowl, with a distinct boutique feel to many of its shops, though larger chains are also represented. ◈ *Map P6 • Mill St • 021 465 1842*

7 Neighbourgoods Market
This deli food market at the revived Old Biscuit Mill is the place to mingle with hip Capetonians on Saturday mornings. The vintage market on Sunday sells clothes, furniture and more. ◈ *Map I1 • Open 9am–2pm Sat & Sun*

8 Milnerton Flea Market
This eclectic flea market is a good bet for shopping on Sundays, when other malls and markets tend to be quiet. ◈ *021 551 7879 • Open Sat, Sun and some public holidays*

9 Canal Walk
Comparable in scale to the V&A Waterfront, this vast complex of shops, cinemas and restaurants is linked to the city by a shuttle bus from popular hotels. ◈ *Map R5 • 021 529 9699 • www.canalwalk.co.za*

10 Church Street Market
Stalls offer a hit and miss assortment, from bric-a-brac to antiques, vintage clothes, costume jewellery, china and old books. ◈ *Map P4 • Open 9am–4pm Mon–Sat*

When browsing in the markets, be alert and avoid carrying more cash than you are likely to need.

63

Left **Cape Town Carriage tour** Right **A wine-tasting tour at Boschendal Wine Estate**

Organized Activities & Day Tours

Cape Town Carriage
This horse-drawn carriage tours historic Cape Town, departing from the Castle of Good Hope and trotting to the Company's Garden and surrounding museums. *021 704 6908 • Departures 10:30am, 12:45pm & 2:45pm (booking required)*

Inverdoorn Game Reserve
This magnificent reserve is a 2.5-hour drive from Cape Town, in the stunning Karoo. Home to an abundance of wildlife, including white rhino and a range of facilities and activities *(see p43)*.

Wine-Tasting Tour
The ideal way to enjoy wine-tasting is through the organized tours of the Winelands available out of Cape Town, Stellenbosch and Franschhoek *(see p106)*.

Cape of Good Hope Day Tour
Organized tours to magnificent Cape Point also take in the Boulders Penguin Colony and include stops along the Atlantic seaboard.

District Six and Townships Tour
A typical day tour starts with a visit to the District Six Museum or the Bo-Kaap, then moves on to the Langa and Khayelitsha townships. Lunch is at a local eatery or *shebeen* (bar). Cape Capers offers several variations. *021 448 3117 • www.tourcapers.co.za*

Robben Island
Probably the most popular organized excursion out of Cape Town is a guided tour of Robben Island, which includes the return boat trip from Nelson Mandela Gateway at the V&A Waterfront *(see pp12–13)*.

Whale and Dolphin Watching Cruise
Best undertaken in calm weather, cetacean-viewing excursions into Table Bay – though not as certain to produce whales as Hermanus – can be organized through kiosks lining the harbour at the V&A Waterfront.

Kloofing
Kloofing (literally "cliffing") is a popular local activity that involves leaping off cliffs into pools in mountain streams of the Winelands. Day trips entail a hike to the *kloofing* site *(see p49)*.

Table Bay Helicopter Trips
Several companies based at the V&A Waterfront offer thrilling helicopter trips with superb aerial views over Table Mountain and the city *(see p48)*.

Table Mountain Day Hike
Experienced hikers will enjoy the hiking possibilities offered at Table Mountain. They are best undertaken with a knowledgeable local guide to avoid being trapped by sudden weather changes. *Cape Eco-Tours • 021 919 2282 • www.cape-ecotours.co.za*

For local day tours and trips further afield, contact Ashworth Africa Tours & Safaris: www.ashworthafrica.com.

Left **Grand Café and Beach** Centre **Bascule Whisky and Wine Bar** Right **Joburg Bar**

🔟 Bars and Cafés

1 Joburg Bar
One of Long Street's longest serving party spots, Joburg Bar is popular for its foot-tapping music and affordable drinks.
◈ *Map P5 • 218 Long St • 021 422 0142*

2 Asoka
Located in an elegant Victorian town house, this stylish and intimate bar will tempt you with delicious cocktails and tasty tapas. ◈ *Map N6 • 68 Kloof St • 021 422 0909*

3 Grand Café and Beach
Enjoy a café-style dining experience on the deck or on the private beach with magnificent views of the ocean. ◈ *Map P1 • Haul Road, Granger Bay • 021 425 0551*

4 Bascule Whisky and Wine Bar
South Africa's largest selection of whiskies, a good wine list, beer on tap and whisky-tasting evenings (book 24 hours ahead) are the main draws of this waterfront bar. ◈ *Map Q2 • Cape Grace, The V&A Waterfront • 021 410 7082*

5 Ferryman's Tavern
Originally a Victorian warehouse, this tavern re-creates an English pub ambience and has beer on tap. You can sit outdoors on warm nights. ◈ *Map P2 • Dock Road, V&A Waterfront • 021 419 7748*

6 Sky Bar & Daddy Cool
Have a drink at the Sky Bar on the rooftop terrace of the Grand Daddy Hotel, which offers seven Silver Bullet Airstream trailers for accommodation with a difference. Downstairs is the glitzy Daddy Cool Bar, where the decor is kitsch but still cool. ◈ *Map P4 • 38 Long St • 021 424 7247*

7 Beerhouse on Long
Enjoy Cape Town's biggest selection of local, international and craft beers in a relaxing environment. ◈ *Map P5 • 223 Long Street • 021 424 3370*

8 Neighbourhood Restaurant, Bar & Lounge
A great gastropub with a games room, large screens showing sporting events and a balcony overlooking Long Street. ◈ *Map P4 • 163 Long Street • 021 424 7260*

9 The Sidewalk Cafe
Mingle with a diverse crowd and enjoy lazy breakfasts, leisurely lunches, sundowners or dinner. ◈ *Map H1 • 33 Derry St, Vredehoek • 021 461 2839*

10 Planet Bar
A sophisticated crowd frequent this bar at the Mount Nelson Hotel for after-work and pre-dinner drinks. Outdoor tables over-look the manicured grounds. ◈ *Map P6 • 76 Orange St • 021 483 1948*

Left **Musician at Mama Africa** Centre **Zula Sound Bar** Right **Fine dining at Shimmy Beach Club**

TOP 10 Music Venues and Nightclubs

1 Mama Africa
Traditional music accompanies an excellent pan-African menu and lively contemporary African decor at this legendary bar and restaurant. ◎ Map P5 • 178 Long St • 021 426 1017

2 Zula Sound Bar
This Long Street favourite hosts live music most nights, with acts ranging from local and international rock to more relaxed acoustic sessions. ◎ Map P5 • 98 Long St • 021 424 2442 • www.zulabar.co.za

3 DecoDance
Cape Town's busiest nightclub plays rock and pop music from the 60s to the 90s. There are monthly theme parties. No entry for under-22s. ◎ Map L3 • 120 Main Rd, Sea Point • 021 433 2912

4 The Assembly
At the forefront of the city's underground music scene with a mix of local and international acts. ◎ Map Q5 • 61 Harrington Street • 021 465 7286

5 ThirtyOne Cape Town
Admire panoramic views of Cape Town from this nightclub on the 31st floor. It attracts a mature (25+) clientele. Guest list and reservations required on Saturdays. ◎ Map Q4 • 31st Floor, ABSA Centre, 2 Riebeek St • 021 421 0581

6 Shimmy Beach Club
A hip nightclub, this also doubles as a fine dining destination in the daytime. It offers live music and unparalleled views of the glittering Atlantic Ocean from an expansive beach deck on the Foreshore. ◎ Map R1 • South Arm Rd, V&A Waterfront • 021 200 7778 • www.shimmybeachclub.com

7 Fiction DJ Bar and Lounge
Great local DJs create a vibrant atmosphere with different music nights Tuesday to Saturday. Tiny dancefloor. ◎ Map P5 • 226 Long Street • hello@fictionbar.com

8 The Concept Cape Town
Just off trendy Long Street, The Concept is an upmarket club in the Central Business District with three dance arenas under one roof. ◎ Map P5 • 6 Pepper St • 079 893 8137 • www.theconceptct.co.za

9 Crew Bar
A vibrant gay bar offering top local music acts, stylish decor and attractive bartenders. It has a dance floor, VIP bar and open verandahs. ◎ Map P3 • 30 Napier St, Green Point • 021 418 0118

10 Dizzy's Cigar Bar and Pub
Live bands play covers at this lively venue. A DJ plays on after the band has finished its set. ◎ Map N6 • 39 & 41 The Drive, Camps Bay • 021 438 2686 • www.dizzys.co.za

Most of the listed music venues post details of upcoming live acts on their website.

Left **A performance at Artscape Theatre Centre** Right **Madame Zingara's travelling theatre**

10 Theatre and Entertainment

Artscape Theatre Centre
Cape Town's premier performing arts complex hosts ballet, opera and cabaret performances. ⊗ *Map R4 • DF Malan St • 021 410 9800 • www.artscape.co.za*

Labia Cinema
This art cinema, named after its benefactor, Princess Labia, shows quality commercial movies and special interest films. ⊗ *Map N6 • 68 Orange St • 021 424 5927 • www.thelabia.co.za*

Little Theatre Complex
The drama department of the University of Cape Town (UCT) stages its student productions at the 230-seat Little Theatre. ⊗ *Map P6 • 37 Orange St • 021 480 7129 • www.littletheatre. uct.ac.za*

GrandWest
This 24-hour wonderland of fun, food and fabulous family entertainment is the largest destination of its kind in South Africa. It includes a theatre, ice rink, cinemas and casino.
⊗ *Map B2 • Vanguard Dr, Goodwood • 021 505 7777*

City Hall
The impressive golden-brick Italian Renaissance-style City Hall is the main concert venue for the Cape Philharmonic Orchestra.
⊗ *Map Q5 • Darling St • www.cpo.org.za*

Madame Zingara's Theatre of Dreams
A spellbinding travelling dinner theatre extravaganza in a magnificent Baroque tent. ⊗ *Map P1 • V&A Waterfront • 0861 623 263 • www.madamezingara.com*

Theatre on the Bay
Stand-up comedy, musicals and conventional farces are the staple of this charming theatre. ⊗ *Map G1 • 1A Link St, Camps Bay • 021 438 3300 • www.theatreonthebay.co.za*

Kirstenbosch Summer Sunset Concerts
Enjoy a picnic at sunset while listening to the open-air concerts (rock to big band) in the beautiful botanical gardens. ⊗ *Map H2 • Rhodes Avenue, Newlands • 021 761 2866*

Baxter Theatre
The Baxter has long been at the cutting edge of local theatre, particularly during the 1980s when it openly defied apartheid laws.
⊗ *Map J1 • 021 685 7880 • Main Rd, Rondebosch • www.baxter.co.za*

The Fugard
Named after South Africa's most famous contemporary playwright, Athol Fugard, Cape Town's world-class theatre, bioscope and events complex is located within historic District Six. ⊗ *Map Q5 • 7 Caledon St • 021 461 4554 • www.thefugard.com*

Left **Sevruga** Centre **Den Anker Restaurant & Bar** Right **Belthazar Restaurant & Wine Bar**

🔟 Eateries at the V&A Waterfront

Willoughby & Co
Seafood is the speciality at this informal venue on Victoria Wharf. It is particularly notable for its sushi and the selection of wines by the glass. ✪ *Map Q1 • 021 418 6115 • RRRRR*

Nobu
Nobu offers a memorable culinary experience in an exclusive setting. Sample classic Japanese cuisine with a modern touch. The black cod den miso is a masterpiece.✪ *Map P2 • One&Only Hotel, V&A Waterfront • 021 431 4511 • RRRRR*

Sevruga
A large and varied menu, of good quality dishes and an extensive wine list of mainly local producers. The staff are often too relaxed but always friendly. ✪ *Map Q5 • Shop 4, Quay 5 • 021 421 5134 • RRRRR*

Baia Seafood Restaurant
This stylishly decorated restaurant serves top-notch seafood, game, meat and poultry dishes, best enjoyed on the terraces with uninterrupted views of Table Mountain. ✪ *Map Q1 • 021 421 0935 • RRRRR*

Den Anker Restaurant and Bar
This stands out from the crowd for its great seafront location and high-ceilinged interior. Belgian specialities such as mussels, rabbit and Belgian beer are served. ✪ *Map P2 • 021 419 0249 • RRR*

Belthazar Restaurant & Wine Bar
Belthazar is a multiple award-winning steakhouse specializing in meat and poultry and claims to have the world's longest by-the-glass wine list. ✪ *Map Q1 • 021 421 3753 • RRRRR*

Panama Jacks
Venturing into the seedy working docks of Cape Town and finding this old shack of a restaurant is an adventure. Choose lobster or abalone from seawater tanks for your supper. Take a taxi. ✪ *Map Q2 • Quay 500, Cape Town Harbour • 021 448 1080 • RRRR*

Quay Four
Two dining choices are on offer here. The Tavern offers pub fare, wooden tables and benches at the water's edge; or a more elegant option is Upstairs at Quay Four. ✪ *Map P1 • 021 419 2008 • RRRR*

Greek Fisherman
Perennial favourite serving seafood and meats grilled over open coals. Sushi and cocktail bars create a lively atmosphere, and the view is amazing. ✪ *Map Q1 • Victoria Wharf, V&A Waterfront • 021 418 5411 • RRRRR*

The Quarterdeck
Traditional Cape Malay, Malaysian, Indonesian and South African fare. The 3-course Chef's Feast is highly recommended. ✪ *Map P2 • 021 418 3281 • RRRR*

Price Categories

For a three-course meal for one, including half a bottle of wine, cover charge, taxes and extra charges.

R	under R150
RR	R150–200
RRR	R200–250
RRRR	R250–300
RRRRR	over R300

Savoy Cabbage

🔟 Restaurants

Planet Restaurant
1 The Mount Nelson Hotel is one of Cape Town's grand dames, and while the stuffy colonialism is gone, elegance remains. A celestial theme dominates, with star-shaped chandeliers dripping with crystals. A South African twist on international cuisine satisfies a 5-star clientele. ✆ *Map P6 • 76 Orange St • 021 483 1000 • RRRRR*

Savoy Cabbage
2 A historic setting, funky interior and imaginative menu make Savoy Cabbage one of Cape Town's hottest eateries. ✆ *Map P4 • 101 Hout St • 021 424 2626 • RRRRR*

Aubergine Restaurant
3 This restaurant serves meat, seafood and vegetarian dishes with African, Asian and European influences. ✆ *Map P6 • 39 Barnet St, Gardens • 021 465 0000 • RRRRR*

Bukhara
4 Cape Town's top Indian restaurant has a varied vegetarian selection on its menu. ✆ *Map Q5 • 33 Church St • 021 424 0000 • RRRRR*

Beluga
5 Tucked away in the office district of Green Point, Beluga offers Eastern-influenced grills, seafood and fantastic value sushi. ✆ *Map H1 • The Foundry, Prestwich St • 021 418 2948 • RRR*

Africa Café
6 A nightly buffet of pan-African dishes make this an excellent option for sampling the varied flavours of the continent. ✆ *Map P4 • 108 Shortmarket St • 021 422 0221 • RRRRR*

Haiku
7 Exotic Asian food is presented tapas-style, so the more people, the more dishes you can try. An open kitchen allows you to watch the artful preparation of your food. ✆ *Map P4 • 58 Burg St • (021) 424 7000 • RR*

Cape Malay Food Market
8 This strictly *halal* eatery in trendy Cape Quarter, renowned for its spicy and aromatic curries, has friendly staff and a laid-back atmosphere. ✆ *Map P3 • 72 Waterkant St, Green Point • 021 418 2299 • RR*

Blues
9 A fixture on Camps Bay for 15 years, this perennial favourite has an adventurous menu of Italian-influenced seafood and meat dishes. ✆ *Map N6 • The Promenade, Victoria Rd, Camps Bay • 021 438 2040 • RRRRR*

Royale Eatery
10 Get your gourmet burger fix from a choice of over 50. Very popular during peak times. ✆ *Map P5 • 273 Long St • 021 422 4536 • RR*

Left **Steenberg Wine Estate** Right **Shacks fronting new buildings at Langa Township**

Southern Suburbs

CAPE TOWN'S MOST SIGNIFICANT CLUSTER *of suburban attractions lies amidst the prestigious belt of leafy residential property that stretches southward from the city centre, flanked to the west by Table Mountain and to the east by the incongruously poor Cape Flats. An area of interest for nature lovers, Kirstenbosch and Tokai offer scenic surroundings for a stroll. The*

estates along the Constantia Wine Route are as enjoyable as its more far-flung counterparts around Stellenbosch. For art lovers, the Irma Stern Museum is a cultural high-light, while sports fans can take in a rugby or cricket match at the world-class Newlands Stadia.

Protea blooms at Kirstenbosch National Botanical Garden

Sights

1. Rhodes Memorial
2. Irma Stern Museum
3. Newlands Rugby Stadium and Cricket Ground
4. Kirstenbosch National Botanical Garden
5. Groot Constantia
6. Klein Constantia
7. Tokai Plantation and Arboretum
8. Steenberg Wine Estate
9. Buitenverwachting Wine Estate
10. Cape Flats Townships

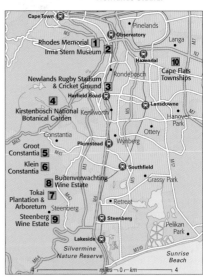

Preceding pages **Kirstenbosch National Botanical Garden**

Rhodes Memorial

Rhodes Memorial
One-time prime minister of the Cape and founder of the Rhodesias (now Zimbabwe and Zambia) *(see p35)*, CJ Rhodes has a memorial dedicated to him on a lookout point below Devil's Peak, which offers memorable views across the Cape Flats. The monument has Neo-Classical aspirations with its Doric columns and stone lions modelled on Nelson's Column. ✪ *Map H1 • 021 687 0000 • Restaurant: open 9am–5pm daily • www.rhodesmemorial.co.za*

Irma Stern Museum
This underrated museum opened in 1971 in the house where versatile artist Irma Stern lived till her death in 1966. Trained in Germany, Stern's impressionist portraits gained international acclaim, but her idealized rendition of African subjects provoked controversy at home. As well as her paintings, the museum also houses Stern's collection of Africana, notably an early 20th-century Congolese stool. ✪ *Map H1 • Cecil Rd, Rosebank • 021 685 5686 • Open 10am–5pm Tue–Fri; 10am–2pm Sat • Adm • www.irmastern.co.za*

Newlands Rugby Stadium and Cricket Ground
Newlands hosted its first international rugby test in 1891. A multipurpose venue with a crowd capacity of 51,900, it is home to one of South Africa's Super Rugby teams *(see p46)*. Nearby, towering Table Mountain looms over the scenic Newlands Cricket Ground. ✪ *Map J2*

Kirstenbosch National Botanical Garden
South Africa's most beautiful botanical garden extends up to the eastern slopes of Table Mountain. It boasts a rich selection of flora and birdlife typical to the Western Cape. The network of wide footpaths, suitable for wheelchair users, forms a springboard for visitors to explore the *fynbos*-draped upper slopes of Table Mountain *(see pp20–21).*

The studio at Irma Stern Museum

Groot Constantia Estate
5 South Africa's oldest wine estate is situated in the suburb of Constantia, below the eastern contours of Table Mountain. The opportunity to taste the award-winning wines alone justifies a visit, as does the stately Manor House *(see pp22–3)*.

Klein Constantia Estate
6 A subdivision of the original Van der Stel estate, Klein Constantia is arguably the finest wine producer in Constantia. Of note is the Vin de Constance, a re-creation of the natural, sweet dessert wine whose ancestral namesake was a favourite with Napoleon Bonaparte. ◈ *Map H2*
• *Klein Constantia Rd* • *021 794 5188*
• *Tasting: 10am–4pm Mon–Fri, 10am–4:30pm Sat* • *www.kleinconstantia.co.za*

Tokai Plantation and Arboretum
7 Incorporated into Table Mountain National Park, this pine tree plantation encloses a Victorian arboretum. Popular with bird-watchers, its winged residents include the forest buzzard and Verreaux's eagle. ◈ *Map H3*
• *Tokai Rd, Tokai* • *021 712 7471* • *Open 8am–4pm daily* • *Adm* • *www.sanparks.org*

Steenberg Wine Estate
8 Located on the oldest farm in the Constantia Valley and set below the eponymous "Stone Mountain", Steenberg was

Buitenverwachting Wine Estate

Manor House Museum in Groot Constantia

established in 1682 as Swaaneweide by Catharina Ras. Its award-winning wines are headed by a superb Sauvignon Blanc reserve and a red blend bearing Catharina's name. The estate has a championship golf course attached. ◈ *Map H3*
• *Steenberg Rd* • *021 713 2211* • *Tasting: 10am–5:55pm daily; cellar tours: call ahead* • *www.steenberg-vineyards.co.za*

Buitenverwachting Wine Estate
9 Translated as "Beyond Expec-tations"– an allusion to the 100-tonne grape harvest reaped by Ryk Cloete in 1825 – this 18th-century Cape Dutch homestead is set at the foot of Constantia Mountain. Though the flagship wine is a Bordeaux-style blend (Christine), the estate also produces unblended reds and whites. There is a restaurant on-site. ◈ *Map H3* • *Klein Constantia Rd, Constantia* • *021 794 5190* • *Tasting 9am–5pm Mon–Fri, 10am–3pm Sat*
• *www.buitenverwachting.co.za*

Cape Flats Townships
10 Practically uninhabited until the 1940s, the sandy flats on the east of the peninsula were urbanized after forced relocation of locals from "Whites Only" suburbs to townships such as Khayelitsha, Langa and Gugulethu. Despite upliftment, poverty is still high. ◈ *Map I1*

Price Categories

For a three course meal for one, including half a bottle of wine, cover charge, taxes and extra charges.

R	under R150
RR	R150–200
RRR	R200–250
RRRR	R250–300
RRRRR	over R300

Jonkershuis Restaurant

🔟 Restaurants

Myoga
Lunch outdoors in the leafy gardens with Table Mountain etched against the skyline, or indoors in the Art Deco-inspired restaurant. The food is a fusion of eastern and western cuisine. ◎ *Map H2 • The Vineyard Hotel, 60 Colinton Rd, Newlands • 021 657 4545 • RRRRR*

The Cape Malay Experience
Cape Town's leading purveyor of spicy Cape Malay cuisine is situated in the historic Cellars-Hohenort Hotel. ◎ *Map H2 • 93 Brommersvlei Rd, Constantia • 021 794 2137 • RRRRR*

Jonkershuis Restaurant
This cozy favourite set on Groot Constantia offers a Cape Malay menu. Unusually, lunch is pricier than the well-priced evening buffets. ◎ *Map H2 • Groot Constantia • 021 794 6255 • RRRR*

Magica Roma
Book ahead at this suburban Italian restaurant. Expect good, consistent fare that warms the heart and doesn't hurt the pocket. ◎ *Map I1 • 8 Central Square, Pinelands • 021 531 1489 • RRRR*

Buitenverwachting Restaurant
An award-winning Winelands restaurant that combines continental and local influences. Picnic baskets should be booked in advance. ◎ *Map H2 • Buitenverwachting Klein Constantia Rd • 021 794 3522 • RRRRR*

The Raj
This popular restaurant attracts a varied crowd with its North Indian cuisine, offering crowd pleasers such as chicken vindaloo and butter chicken. ◎ *Map H2 • Shop 17, Old Village, Constantia Shopping Centre • 021 794 6546 • RRR*

Moyo Kirstenbosch
Conveniently located in the Kirstenbosch National Botanical Garden, Moyo's menu is supplemented by filled pancakes and sandwiches. Picnic baskets must be pre-booked (see p20). • *RRRR*

Constantia Uitsig Restaurant
Set on the Uitsig Wine Estate, this restaurant matches a variety of South African and Italian dishes with the estate's acclaimed wines. ◎ *Map H2 • Constantia Uitsig Estate, Spaanschemat River Rd • 021 794 4480 • RRRRR*

La Colombe
This Uitsig institution in an airy Cape Dutch building serves superlative French and fusion cuisine and top-notch Cape and French wines. ◎ *Map H2 • Constantia Uitsig Estate, Spaanschemat River Rd • 021 794 2390 • RRRRR*

Bistro Sixteen82
The bistro and tapas menu raises the standard of casual dining to an art form, without breaking the bank. ◎ *Map H3 • Steenberg Estate, Steenberg Rd, Tokai • 021 713 2211 • RRRR*

For more restaurants in and around Cape Town, see pp52–3, 81, 90–91, 99.

Left **Fishing boats at Hout Bay harbour** Right **Hout Bay as seen from Chapman's Peak Drive**

The Cape Peninsula

THE CAPE PENINSULA IS A MOUNTAINOUS SLIVER OF LAND *that extends southward from Cape Town to Cape Point, flanked by the open Atlantic to the west and False Bay to the east. Two-thirds of the coastline along the north of the peninsula is studded with quaint villages, sandy beaches and pretty seaside resorts. However, the ragged mountain spine remains largely unsettled, supporting a cover of unspoilt fynbos interspersed with plantation forest. Most of the peninsula is protected within Table Mountain National Park (TMNP). Outdoor enthusiasts living in Cape Town will testify to the opportunities that TMNP presents; you could spend a lifetime exploring this scenic tract of land, but for time-bound tourists, highlights in the*

peninsula include the Cape of Good Hope sector of TMNP (see pp26–7), the entertaining penguin colony residents at Boulders Beach near Simon's Town, and the lovely beaches at Muizenberg, Noordhoek and Fish Hoek.

Scarlet Ibis at World of Birds

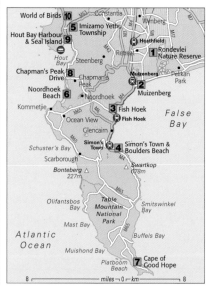

Sights

1. Rondevlei Nature Reserve
2. Muizenberg
3. Fish Hoek
4. Simon's Town and Boulders Beach
5. Imizamo Yethu Township
6. Noordhoek Beach
7. Cape of Good Hope
8. Chapman's Peak Drive
9. Hout Bay Harbour and Seal Island
10. World of Birds

Sunbathers at Fish Hoek beach

Fish Hoek

The quaint village of Fish Hoek lies at the mouth of the Silvermine River between Muizenberg and Simon's Town, and boasts one of the warmest and safest swimming beaches on the Peninsula. The clifftop Jager's Path runs southward from town and offers good vantage points for whale watching. Overlooking the town is Peers Cave, one of the Cape's most important archaeological sites and a national monument. It contains evidence of human occupation dating back 11,000 years. ◈ Map H4

Rondevlei Nature Reserve

A short drive north of Muizenberg, Rondevlei – Cape Town's best bird sanctuary – is home to 230 marine and fresh-water species, which can be glimpsed from the short walking trail that connects its hides. Grebes, rails, herons and gulls are well represented here. Hippos were introduced in 1982 to control the spread of surface vegetation. ◈ Map J3 • Perth Rd, Rondevlei • 021 706 2404 • Open 7:30am–5pm daily; Dec–Feb: 7:30am–5pm Mon–Fri, 7:30am–7pm Sat & Sun • Adm

Muizenberg

This resort town on False Bay was the location chosen a century ago by Witwatersrand gold magnates to build a row of seafront mansions. Though less prestigious now, the town's historical sights include Het Posthuys, built as a tollhouse in 1742, the battlements, which are remnants of the 1795 Anglo-Dutch Battle of Muizenberg, the Edwardian railway station and Rhodes Cottage Museum, where CJ Rhodes died in 1902. The wide, sheltered beach is a haven for surfers and swimmers. ◈ Map J3

Simon's Town and Boulders Beach

A naval base for over 200 years, the pleasantly time-warped feel of Simon's Town is enhanced by the "Historic Mile", a row of Victorian façades lining St George's Street. The town's Victorian railway station is the southern terminus of one of the world's great suburban train rides. The route follows the False Bay seafront back to Muizenberg. The penguin colony south of the town centre at Boulders Beach is the main attraction (see pp24–5).

Muizenberg's beachfront

Cape Floral Kingdom

The smallest of the world's six floral kingdoms, the Cape consists of a unique floral community known as *fynbos* ("fine bush"), a reference to the narrow leaves of many plants. A UNESCO World Heritage Site and a biodiversity hotspot for its floral wealth, the Cape Peninsula supports more indigenous species than the entire British Isles.

Shacks on the mountainside, Imizamo Yethu

Imizamo Yethu Township

This name is an isiXhosa phrase meaning "Through Collective Struggle". This small township was established on the outskirts of Hout Bay after the collapse of apartheid in the 1990s. The township's picturesque setting overlooking the harbour is offset in shocking contrast by the harsh living conditions endured by its 25,000 residents. Township Tours SA provides tours into Imizamo Yethu. ◈ *Map G2 • Township Tours SA: 083 719 4870; 10:30am, 1pm, 4pm daily*

Noordhoek Beach

An expanse of bone-white sand running from the base of Chapman's Peak to Kommetjie,

Noordhoek is the most beautiful beach on the Cape Peninsula. It is a lovely spot for walks and birdwatching; you may even catch a glimpse of the endangered black oystercatcher. Horse riding is also on offer here *(see p46)*. ◈ *Map G3*

Cape of Good Hope

This reserve is the scenic highlight of the Peninsula, dotted with stunning viewpoints such as Rooikrans, Gifkommetjie and Cape Point. It is an important stronghold for the Cape's unique *fynbos* habitat and for wildlife such as the eland and the endemic bontebok *(see pp26–7)*.

Chapman's Peak Drive

Named after the peak that soars above it, Chapman's Peak Drive, constructed in 1915–22, is a magnificent stretch of road. Excavated into a band of soft shale in the almost-vertical cliff face that connects Hout Bay to Noordhoek, the road runs past parking spots from where you can watch the Atlantic batter the cliff's base. It now operates as a toll road after years of repair work. ◈ *Map G3*

The shores of Noordhoek Beach

9 Hout Bay Harbour and Seal Island

Hout Bay's busy little harbour is the launching point for boat trips to Seal Island, a flat granite outcrop that lies about 6 km (4 miles) offshore. The island's rocky shores support up to 75,000 Cape fur seals, the largest colony in South Africa. People are forbidden from landing on the island, but plenty of seals can be seen from the boat, together with various marine birds including black oystercatchers, African penguins and breeding colonies of three different cormorant species.
⊗ Map G3 • Hout Bay • Tours every hour

Reposing seals on Seal Island

10 World of Birds

In a leafy suburb of Hout Bay, the World of Birds houses around 400 species, from indigenous garden birds such as bulbuls and parrots, to spectacular exotic species such as the scarlet ibis and Indian peacock. It also has an important breeding programme for the endangered southern bald ibis and crowned crane. The Monkey Jungle is a walk-through enclosure where mischievous South American squirrel monkeys clamber over you. Other popular residents include baboons and charismatic meerkats. ⊗ Map G2
• Valley Rd, Hout Bay • 021 790 2730
• Adm • www.worldofbirds.org.za

A Full-Day Driving Tour to Cape Point

Morning

After an early breakfast, head down the Atlantic seaboard via Camps Bay. Leave in time to break the 45-minute drive to **Hout Bay** with stops along **Chapman's Peak Drive** to enjoy the view. If you reach Hout Bay before 9:30am, hop aboard a round-trip cruise to **Seal Island**. Then continue your journey, driving south to the **Cape of Good Hope** sector of **Table Mountain National Park** (see p40). Stop at the Buffelsfontein Visitor Centre before you reach the Cape Point car park. If you're already peckish, enjoy a scenic lunch at the **Two Oceans Restaurant** (see p81) overlooking False Bay, or wait until after you've climbed the steep footpath (or caught the funicular) to **Cape Point Lighthouse** (see p27).

Afternoon

Walk off the lunch following the footpath from the car park to the Cape of Good Hope Beach, or drive back along the main road through the reserve towards the entrance gate, diverting to the **Rooikrans**, **Gifkommetjie** and **Platboom Beach**. Leave by 3pm, following the road that hugs the False Bay seaboard towards **Simon's Town** (see p76). Stop occasionally to look out for whales. Before you reach Simon's Town, turn right for **Boulders Beach** (see p76) to watch the squabbling penguins. Before driving back, enjoy a drink at **Seaforth Restaurant** (see p81), or at **Bertha's** (see p81), overlooking Simon's Town's harbour.

Left **Quayside Centre** Right **Curios at the craft stalls, Hout Bay harbour**

Galleries and Shops

Kalk Bay Gallery
1 This gallery specializes in fine art by local artists. You can have your purchase shipped to anywhere in the world. ✆ *Map H4*
• *62 Main Rd, Kalk Bay • 021 788 1674*

Artvark
2 A contemporary art gallery showcasing South African art and craft, it also sells custom and exclusive steelworks. ✆ *Map H4*
• *48 Main Rd, Kalk Bay • 021 788 5584*

Quagga Rare Books & Art
3 This highly regarded anti-quarian bookshop has numerous out-of-print titles. ✆ *Map H4*
• *84 Main Rd, Kalk Bay • 021 788 2752*

Kalk Bay Modern
4 Local modern art, textiles and crafts are featured in this gallery. ✆ *Map H4, 136 Main Rd, Kalk Bay • 021 788 6571*

Quayside Centre
5 A sophisticated complex below Quayside Hotel, the cen-tre boasts curio shops, an art gallery, and eateries overlooking Simon's Town's harbour. ✆ *Map H4*

A sculpture display at Kalk Bay Modern

Sophea Gallery
6 This Tibetan influenced set-up consists of a gallery for spiritual art, a Tibetan Teahouse serving vegetarian and vegan food and a sanctuary for meditation. ✆ *Map H4*
• *2 Harrington Rd, Seaforth • 021 786 1544*

Longbeach Mall
7 The southern peninsula's largest shopping complex contains more than 90 shops including supermarkets, a craft market, restaurants and coffee shops. ✆ *Map H3 • Cnr Buller Louw Dr & Sunnydale Rd, Noordhoek • 021 785 5955*

Ethno Bongo ... & Banana
8 Find quality local wood items with a seaside theme and fabulous jewellery made by hand using organic materials such as shells, beads and gemstones at this original gift shop. ✆ *Map G2 • Main Rd, Hout Bay • 021 790 0802*

Hout Bay Craft Market
9 A row of stalls located in Hout Bay harbour sell local curios, ranging from batiks to beadwork and wooden carvings. ✆ *Map G3*

Rose Korber Art
10 This renowned art dealer has a collection of works by leading contemporary South African artists. Korber also curates an annual exhibition of top contemporary South African art. ✆ *Map H1 • 48 Sedgemoor Rd, Camps Bay • 021 438 9152, 083 261 1173 • www.rosekorberart.com*

Price Categories

For a three course meal for one, including half a bottle of wine, cover charge, taxes and extra charges.

R	under R150
RR	R150–200
RRR	R200–250
RRRR	R250–300
RRRRR	over R300

Bertha's restaurant

🏆10 Restaurants

1 Olympia Café
People queue for the laid-back, seaside atmosphere, shabby chic interior, excellent breakfasts and Mediterranean dishes. 🕾 *Map H3 • 134 Main Rd, Kalk Bay • 021 788 6396 • RRRR*

2 Galley Seafood Restaurant
Also known as the Bayside, this beachfront eatery serves up fresh seafood – the mixed platters are legendary – and a good selection of meat dishes. 🕾 *Map H4 • Fish Hoek Beach • 021 782 3354 • RR*

3 Bertha's
With an attractive location on the Quayside Centre's ground floor, Bertha's serves meat and seafood at good value. 🕾 *Map H4 • Wharf Rd, Simon's Town • 021 786 2138 • RR*

4 Harbour House
This upstairs restaurant is as close to the ocean you can get inside Kalk Bay harbour, with huge glass windows looking out onto the ocean. The understated fine dining includes seafood and meat dishes. 🕾 *Map H3 • Kalk Bay Harbour • 021 788 4133 • RRRRR*

5 Seaforth Restaurant
Ideally combined with a visit to the Boulders Penguin Colony *(see p77)*, this seafood restaurant also serves excellent pasta and pizza dishes. 🕾 *Map H4 • Seaforth Beach, Simon's Town • 021 786 4810 • RRR*

6 Two Oceans Restaurant and Snack Bar
Famed for its fine Cape seafood and sublime sushi, this modern restaurant at Cape Point is also known for its staggering views of False Bay. 🕾 *Map I6 • Cape Point • 021 780 9200 • Closed for dinner • RRRRR*

7 The Foodbarn
Chef Franck Dangereux is a master of taste and flavour. The restaurant reflects French gastronomy, while the deli serves light meals and takeaway pies and quiches. 🕾 *Map G3 • Noordhoek Farm Village, Village Lane, Noordhoek • 021 789 1390 • RRRRR*

8 Lookout Deck
Great harbour views are a feature of this popular restaurant. It serves great seafood platters and affordable snacks. 🕾 *Map G3 • Hout Bay Harbour • 021 790 0900 • RRRRR*

9 Dunes
On the sands of Hout Bay beach, this bistro serves everything from tapas, salad and seafood to steaks and pizzas. It's good for families, and has a children's playground. 🕾 *Map G2 • 1 Beach Rd, Hout Bay • 021 790 1876 • RRR*

10 Azure Restaurant
Set in the prestigious Twelve Apostles Hotel *(see p112)*, this gourmet restaurant combines Cape cuisine with international elements. 🕾 *Map H1 • Victoria Rd, Camps Bay • 021 437 9000 • RRRRR*

Restaurants are open for lunch as well as dinner unless otherwise noted.

Left **Historic house in Stellenbosch** Right **Boschendal Wine Estate**

The Winelands

THE MOUNTAINOUS TERRITORY *immediately inland of Cape Town, often referred to as the Boland (literally "Uplands"), is among the most beautiful parts of South Africa. Its rugged sandstone peaks, interspersed with lush well-watered valleys, support intensive cultivation of deciduous fruit and trees. This region also forms the heart of the country's wine industry; it is home to around 300 different wineries and is well organized for tourism, with most estates offering wine-tasting facilities and many also operating restaurants or cafés. A significant feature of the Winelands is its historic towns, which include Stellenbosch, Franschhoek, Tulbagh and Paarl.*

Vergelegen Wine Estate's wine-tasting lodge

🔟 Sights

1. Stellenbosch
2. Jonkershoek Nature Reserve
3. Spier Wine Farm
4. Boschendal Wine Estate
5. Franschhoek
6. Butterfly World
7. Drakenstein Lion Park
8. Paarl
9. Tulbagh
10. Vergelegen Wine Estate

1 Stellenbosch

The tourist capital of the Winelands lies amidst mountainous surrounds on the banks of the Eerste River. Established just 27 years after Cape Town was settled, Stellenbosch is South Africa's second oldest town and boasts the country's highest

The sandstone mountains of Jonkershoek Nature Reserve

concentration of pre-20th-century Cape Dutch buildings. Despite its overtly historic feel, Stellenbosch is anything but staid, thanks partially to the bustling student life associated with its renowned university. The compact town centre is lively – and very safe – even after dark (see pp28–9).

2 Jonkershoek Nature Reserve

One of the Cape's most overlooked attractions, this mountainous reserve is on the outskirts of Stellenbosch. It is traversed by a selection of hiking trails, ranging from the easy paths through the reclaimed farmland of the Assegaaibosch sector, to the demanding hikes to the upper slopes. The mountain scenery hosts more than 1,000 species of *fynbos* plants and a varied selection of birds. The large mammal population – though thinly distributed – includes leopards, baboons and klipspringers. ✪ *Map E3*
• *Jonkershoek Valley: 021 866 1560; open 8am–4:30pm daily; adm* • *Assegaaibosch: open 8am–4:30pm daily; adm* • *www.capenature.co.za*

3 Spier Wine Farm

This estate does not aim for the gracious winelands ambience of Boschendal or Vergelegen, but

recent upgrades have resulted in a more sophisticated environment, particularly at the newly renovated wine-tasting venue, Eight to Go deli. Excellent facilities ensure that it goes down well with everyone. There are grape juice tasting sessions for those who don't take their wine too seriously. The estate has a spa, playground, craft shop, daily Eagle Encounter shows and the superb four-star Spier Hotel (see p117), with its impressive and modern decor. There are various restaurants and also conference facilities.
✪ *Map D3* • *Off R310 en route Stellenbosch* • *021 809 1100* • *Open 10am–4:30pm daily* • *www.spier.co.za*

4 Boschendal Wine Estate

The pioneering Boschendal Estate was first planted with vines by Huguenot settler Jean de Long in 1685. The most popular in the Stellenbosch-Franschhoek area, this estate is reached via a tree-lined drive and lies in a green valley flanked by the Groot Drakenstein and Simonsberg Mountains. The estate's Cape Dutch architecture includes a manor house dating to 1812 and a cellar built in 1795. There's a classy buffet restaurant and shady café, but on sunny days, the French-style "Le Pique-Nique" on the lawns is irresistible (see p30).

5 Franschhoek

Franschhoek is the self-styled culinary capital of South Africa. With a French influence that dates back to its settlement by Huguenot refugees in the late 17th century, the town's history is documented in the Huguenot Memorial and Museum lying on its outskirts. Many wine estates lie in the immediate vicinity of this small town and its upsurge as a tourist hub is reflected in the boutique shops and world-class restaurants lining the main street *(see pp30–31)*.

6 Butterfly World

Situated in Klapmuts on the R44, Butterfly World is South Africa's largest butterfly park and supports more than 20 indigenous free-flying species in an attractive, landscaped indoor garden. The fascinating Martin Filmer Spider Room, which has many different species of spiders housed in terrariums, educates visitors about the ecological value of these unjustly feared arachnids. ◎ *Map D1 • R44, Klapmuts • 021 875 5628 • Open 9am–5pm daily • Adm*

Butterfly World

Cape Dutch Houses

The Cape Dutch architecture that evolved in the 18th century adapted European styles to suit African conditions. Its defining feature, derived from medieval houses in Amsterdam, is an ornate round gable above the entrance. Typical buildings also have a thatched roof and an H-shaped floor plan like the manor house at Vergelegen.

7 Drakenstein Lion Park

This park provides lifelong sanctuary to 35 lions, two Bengal tigers and various other mammals and birds. People flock here to visit the Chimp Haven and for the chance to sleep overnight in safari tents surrounded by the lions. Feeding time (4pm on Mon, Wed and Fri) is also very popular. ◎ *Map E1 • Old Paarl Rd (R101), Klapmuts • 021 863 3290 • Open 9:30am–5pm daily • Adm • www.lionrescue.org.za*

8 Paarl

Hemmed in by Paarl Mountain to the west and the Berg River to the east, the largest town in the Winelands is rather scruffy compared to Stellenbosch. However, Paarl Mountain, a fantastic granite outcrop in a pedestrian-friendly nature reserve, and the Afrikaner Taal (Language) Monument are worth a visit. The Laborie Wine Estate in the town centre is charming. ◎ *Map E1 • 021 872 4842 • www.paarlonline.com*

A rescued lion at Drakenstein Lion Park

For more details of attractions between Stellenbosch and Franschhoek, **see pp30–31.**

9 Tulbagh

The town of Tulbagh, below the Groot Winterhoek Mountains, was founded in 1700 and is relatively remote from Cape Town. It makes a charming getaway for those who want to avoid crowds. Boasting more than 30 Cape Dutch buildings, the centre exudes a period character. The *fynbos*-draped Groot Winterhoek Mountains form an imposing backdrop and offer good walking, horse riding and birdwatching opportunities. The area supports about two dozen wine estates.

Tourist information: Map U3 • 023 230 1375 • www.tulbaghtourism.co.za

10 Vergelegen Wine Estate

Translated as "lying afar", this historic property on the slopes of the Helderberg started life as a remote outpost of the Cape Colony in 1685. Fifteen years later, it became the private estate of Willem van der Stel, who established the gracious manor house and octagonal garden, and planted the gnarled camphor trees at its entrance. Visit one of South Africa's premier estates for its magnificent grounds or to sample its range of wines.

Map E4 • Lourensford Rd, Somerset West • 021 847 1334 • Tasting 9:30am–4:30pm daily • Adm • www.vergelegen.co.za

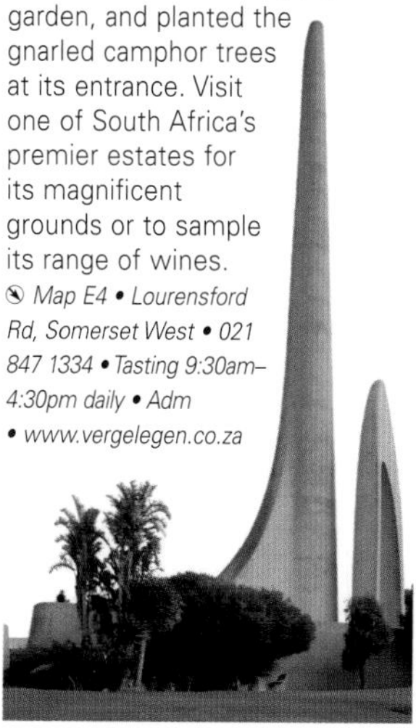

Afrikaner Taal Monument, Paarl

The "Four Passes" Day Circuit

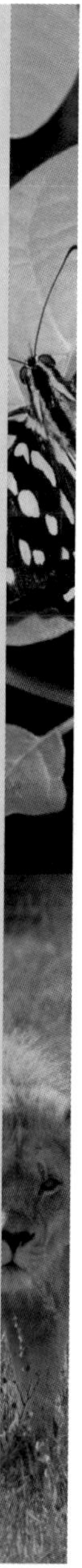

Morning

The circuit around the **Hottentots Holland Mountains** encompasses some of the Winelands' finest scenery, architecture and wine estates. Starting in **Stellenbosch** *(see pp28–9)*, drive south along the R310 to Somerset West. Follow the signs to the **Vergelegen Wine Estate** on the Helderberg slopes. Once here, explore the historic buildings and pause for a quick snack at a local coffee shop. From Somerset West, follow the N2 east via Sir Lowry's Pass, then turn left onto the R321, passing through Grabouw and over Viljoen Pass before descending into the **Riviersonderend** (River Without End) Valley to **Theewaterskloof Dam**. Turn left onto the R45, which traverses the Franschhoek Pass, offering wonderful views over this eponymous town.

Afternoon

In **Franschhoek**, lunch at the Tasting Room at Le Quartier Francais or **Mont Rochelle's** two restaurants *(see p91)*. Then pop into the **Huguenot Memorial and Museum** or browse the shops along the main street. Continue west along the R45 and stop at **L'Ormarins Wine Estate** to visit the **Franschhoek Motor Museum** *(see p30)*. Outside Franschhoek, branch left onto the R310 to reach Stellenbosch via the **Helshoogte Pass**. Stop en route at the **Boschendal Wine Estate** *(see p83)*, the town of Pniel and Hillcrest Berry Farm. End your day with a drink at the Tokara Estate's restaurant *(see p87)*.

Operators in Cape Town and Stellenbosch offer "Four Passes" day tours, preferable to self-driving if you plan on wine-tasting.

Left **Items at Oom Samie se Winkel** Centre **University Art Gallery** Right **Sasol Art Museum**

🔟 Galleries and Shops

1 University of Stellenbosch Art Gallery

Housed in a wooden-floored Lutheran church, this small gallery displays works by contemporary South African artists, including pieces by fine art students from the university. ◈ *Map D2 • Cnr Dorp & Bird Sts • 021 808 3524 • Open 9am–5pm Mon–Fri, 9am–1pm Sat*

2 Sasol Art Museum

This tiered, Neo-Classical building displays the university's collection of 19th- and 20th-century art, along with an anthropological collection of traditional African crafts and household objects. ◈ *Map D2 • 52 Ryneveld St • 021 808 3691 • Open 10am–4:30pm Mon, 9am–4pm Tue–Sat*

3 Rupert Museum

A superb collection of contemporary South African art amassed by Dr Anton Rupert is housed in this gallery *(see p28)*.

4 Local Works Arts & Crafts

This impressive little shop has a collection of handpicked pieces that highlight the diversity of African art and culture. ◈ *Map D2 • 10 Drostdy St, Stellenbosch • 021 887 0875 • www.stellenbosch-unlimited. co.za/localworks*

5 Oom Samie se Winkel

Stellenbosch's most famous *winkel* (shop) is over 100 years old and retains a Victorian appearance. It features an eclectic range of affordable local craftwork and genuine Africana. ◈ *Map D2 • Dorp St • 021 887 0797*

6 Karoo Classics

Handcrafted items made of mohair, ostrich leather and natural materials are the speciality at this shop in the town centre. ◈ *Map D2 • Cnr Bird & Church Sts, Stellenbosch • 021 886 7596 • www.karooclassics.co.za*

7 Is Art Gallery

With its coloured handicrafts, jewellery and candles, this annexe of Le Quartier Français *(see p116)* is a curio hunter's delight. ◈ *Map F2 • Huguenot Rd, Franschhoek • 021 876 2151 • www.is-art.co.za*

8 The Ceramics Gallery

View the beautiful, utilitarian pottery by David Walters and even watch him working at the wheel. ◈ *Map F2 • 24 Dirkie Uys St, Franschhoek • 021 876 4304 • www. davidwalters.co.za*

9 Huguenot Fine Chocolates

Delicious chocolates prepared by two local Belgian-trained chocolatiers are sold at this boutique. ◈ *Map F2 • 62 Huguenot Rd, Franschhoek • 021 876 4096*

10 Vineyard Connection

This shop, between Stellenbosch and Paarl, stocks the Cape's finest wines and even delivers them to your home.◈ *Map D2 • Delvera Wine Estate • 021 884 4360*

Left **Rustenberg Wines** Right **Cellar at Blaauwklippen**

🔟 Wine Estates near Stellenbosch

1 Rust en Vrede
This was the first wine estate to specialize in premium red wines only. Dine in the great restaurant. ⊗ *Map D3 • Annandale Rd, Stellenbosch • 021 881 3881 • 9am–5pm Mon–Sat • www.rustenvrede.com*

2 Rustenberg Wines
This 300-year-old farm is known for its Chardonnays. ⊗ *Map E2 • Lily Rd, Ida's Valley • 021 809 1200 • Tasting 9am–4:30pm Mon–Fri, 10am–4pm Sat, 10am–3pm Sun) • www. rustenberg.co.za*

3 Tokara
Located on Helshoogte Pass, Tokara has a scenically positioned restaurant. As well as its acclaimed wines, it is known for its superb olive oil *(see p30).*

4 Delaire
A "vineyard in the sky" on the crest of Helshoogte Pass, Delaire is a lovely spot for a picnic with chilled wine *(see p30).*

5 Neethlingshof
The Short Story Collection and unblended wines of this estate make it a must for wine lovers. ⊗ *Map D3 • M12 • 021 883 8988 • Tasting 9am–5pm Mon–Fri, 10am–4pm Sat, Sun • www.neethlingshof.co.za*

6 Asara
Asara specializes in red wines; the Cabernet Sauvignon is recommended. ⊗ *Map D3 • M12 • 021 888 8000 • Tasting 10am–6pm Mon–Sat, 10am–4pm Sun*

7 Spier Wine Farm
This estate has mid-priced, very quaffable wines and lots of family-oriented activities on offer *(see p83).*

8 Meerlust
At Meerlust, the cellar is stocked with the iconic claret-style Rubicon blend. ⊗ *Map D3 • R310 • 021 843 3587 • Tasting: 9am–5pm Mon–Fri, 10am–2pm Sat • www.meerlust.co.za*

9 Blaauwklippen
This popular estate is home to a carriage museum and a historic manor house restaurant, and produces a quality Zinfandel. ⊗ *Map D3 • R44 • 021 880 0133 • Tasting 9am–5pm Mon–Fri, 10am–5pm Sat, 10am–4pm Sun • www.blaauwklippen.com*

10 Kanonkop
Apart from several award-winning blends, Kanonkop also produces one of the finest representatives of South Africa's Pinotage. ⊗ *Map D2 • R44 • 021 884 4656 • Tasting 9am–5pm Mon–Fri, 9am–2pm Sat • www.kanonkop.co.za*

For more detailed information on South Africa's speciality wines, see p89.

Left **Vineyards at Durbanville** Centre **Haute Cabrière estate** Right **Wine-tasting group at La Motte**

🔟 Other Wine Estates

1 Durbanville Hills
Visit the Durbanville Hills estate for some excellent Merlots. 🗺 Map C2 • M13, Tygervalley Rd 021 558 1300 • Tasting 9am–4:30pm Mon–Thu, 9am–6pm Fri, 10am–3pm Sat, 11am–3pm Sun • www.durbanvillehills.co.za

2 Vergelegen
If you only visit one estate, make sure to visit Vergelegen – it is the consummate Winelands experience (see p85).

3 Boschendal Wine Estate
This estate is a favourite for its scenery, architecture, wines and picnic baskets (see p83).

4 La Motte
La Motte has a lovely location in the Franschhoek Valley. 🗺 Map F2 • R45 Main Rd, Franschhoek • 021 876 8000 • Tasting 9am–5pm Mon–Sat • www.la-motte.com

5 Haute Cabrière
Haute Cabrière is known for its world-class sparkling wines. The corks are removed with a sword. 🗺 Map F2 • Franschhoek Pass Rd • 021 876 8500 • Tasting 9am–5pm Mon–Fri, 10am–4pm Sat, 11am–4pm Sun • www.cabriere.co.za

6 Laborie
Offering a chic country experience, Laborie is a wine farm in the heart of Paarl that has few equals. 🗺 Map E1 • Taillefer St, Paarl • 021 807 3390 • Tasting 9am–5pm Mon–Sat, 11am–5pm Sun • www.laboriewines.co.za

7 Rhebokskloof
Encircled by mountains, this estate offers leisure and adventure activities. 🗺 Map E1 • Windmeul, Agter Paarl • 021 869 8386 • Tasting 9am–5pm daily • www.rhebokskloof.co.za

8 Fairview
A popular estate, Fairview produces fine wines and has a superb deli that serves hand-crafted cheese. 🗺 Map E1 • Suid Agter-Paarl Rd • 021 863 2450 • Tasting 9am–5pm daily • www.fairview.co.za

9 Vergenoegd
The underrated Vergenoegd can boast award-winning reds. 🗺 Map C3 • Baden Powell Dr, R310 • 021 843 3248 • Tasting 9am–5pm Mon–Fri, 9:30am–4pm Sat & Sun • www.vergenoegd.co.za

10 Zevenwacht
Apart from fine red wines, their facilities include cheese-tasting, wine-pairings and a day spa. 🗺 Map C3 • Langverwacht Rd, Kuils River • 021 900 5700 • Tasting 8:30am–5pm Mon–Fri, 9:30am–5pm Sat–Sun • www.zevenwacht.co.za

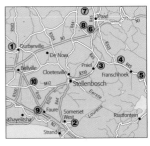

➡ *Most estates charge a tasting fee of between R20 and R50, which typically allows you to try about 6 wines.*

Left **Tasting room at the Meerlust estate** Right **Kanonkop wine estate**

🔟 Iconic Wines to Try

1 Kanonkop Paul Sauer
This is one of South Africa's most celebrated Bordeaux blends, led always by Cabernet Sauvignon. It has a restrained style and is medium-bodied, with well-judged oak.

2 Beyerskloof Pinotage Reserve
This wine is made from South Africa's 'own' grape, created in the early 1920s by crossing Pinot Noir with Cinsaut (known as Hermitage). Beyers Truter's name is synonymous with Pinotage, and this is a particularly good one.

3 Meerlust Rubicon
A true icon established in 1693 and owned by the Myburgh family since 1756, this is one of South Africa's first and best-known Bordeaux blends, with several awards to its name.

4 Boekenhoutskloof Syrah
This wine made Marc Kent's reputation in the wine industry with his first harvest in 1997. Now an industry benchmark, it leans towards Old World styling but is proudly individual.

5 Hamilton Russell Vineyards Pinot Noir
This property in the Hemel-en-Aarde Valley pioneered Pinot Noir in South Africa in the 1970s. Juxtaposing power and restraint, its typical raspberry/cherry core is always well-wrapped in assertive yet controlled tannins.

6 Beaumont Hope Marguerite Chenin Blanc
Chenin Blanc is the South African industry's workhorse and finds its way into sparkling wines, dry table wines, sweet wines and brandy. It is smooth, fruitful but serious, with reined-in oaking.

7 Cape Point Isliedh
Located in the teeth of the Cape's notorious wind where only white grapes reach full ripeness, this is a white Bordeaux blend in which Sauvignon Blanc's stone fruit and herbs are enhanced by Sémillon and a touch of new oak.

8 Ken Forrester The FMC Chenin Blanc
As extravagant and outgoing a Chenin Blanc as Ken Forrester himself, this wine is individualistic, complex, sweet on entry but with enough tang to finish long and dry.

9 The House of Krone Borealis Cuvée Brut
This is the historic homestead, established in 1710, where Nicky Krone helped found the Cape's bottle-fermented sparkling wine industry. His Borealis Cuvée Brut is a sentimental favourite of many.

10 Nederburg Edelkeur Noble Late Harvest
The first Cape Noble Late Harvest (always made from Chenin Blanc), this wine exudes melon and apricot flavours, while limy acidity seams the sweetness and converts it into delicious nectar.

Left **Terroir** Right **Eight at Spier Wine Farm**

TOP 10 Restaurants Around Stellenbosch

1 The Wijnhuis
With a cellar-like decor, this first-floor restaurant has one of the most extensive wine lists in Stellenbosch. It specializes in Mediterranean seafood and grills. ॐ *Map D2 • Cnr Church & Andringa • 021 887 5844 • RRRR*

2 Volkskombuis
Set in authentic Cape Dutch surroundings, this restaurant specializes in traditional cuisine. On the same property, De Oewer, with its Mediterranean menu, is a touch cheaper. ॐ *Map D2 • Aan-de-Wagen Rd • 021 887 2121 • RRRR*

3 Liefde Bistro
This courtyard restaurant at Oude Werf has a small but imaginative menu of Malay dishes, seafood and game, and a good wine list. ॐ *Map D2 • 30 Church St • 021 887 4608 • RRRRR*

4 Bukhara Restaurant
This superb North Indian restaurant with an extensive menu is particularly strong on tandoori dishes. ॐ *Map D2 • Cnr Dorp & Bird • 021 882 9133 • RRRRR*

5 Tokara Delicatessen
A good-value country menu with a healthy spin, using Tokara's own olive oils, farm produce, artisanal cheeses and charcuterie. Great for a weekend brunch (not open for dinner). For fine dining try Tokara Restaurant. ॐ *Map E2 • Tokara Estate, Helshoogte Pass • 021 808 5950 • RR–RRR*

6 Babel at Babylonstoren
A simple menu reflects the colours and tastes of the season. Fruit, vegetables and herbs are gathered daily from the enormous period gardens. ॐ *Map D2 • Babylonstoren Estate, Klapmuts/Simondium Rd, Simondium • 021 863 3852 • RRRR*

7 Spier Wine Farm
This estate has many restaurants. Eight serves dishes buffet-style, while Eight to Go deli has a range of ready-to-eat options. The Spier Hotel Restaurant offers à la carte dining, and Moyo has a pan-African feel. ॐ *Map D3 • Lynedoch Rd, Stellenbosch • 021 809 1152 • RR–RRRRR*

8 96 Winery Road
This country-style restaurant has a changing menu of seasonal dishes. It also has a private cellar of vintage Cape reds. ॐ *Map D4 • Winery Rd (off the R44), Somerset West • 021 842 2020 • RRR*

9 Jordan
Thanks to Jordan's location in the Cape Winelands countryside, the flavours of the locally sourced food are intense, as is the view of the vineyards stretching to the horizon. ॐ *Map D2 • Kloof Rd • 021 881 3612 • RRRRR*

10 Terroir
Set on the Kleine Zalze Estate, this restaurant's changing Provençal-style chalkboard menu combines French and local influences. ॐ *Map D3 • Kleine Zalze Wine Estate • 021 880 8167 • RRRRR*

Credit and debit cards are accepted at all restaurants.

Price Categories

For a three course meal for one, including half a bottle of wine, cover charge, taxes and extra charges.

R	under R150
RR	R150–200
RRR	R200–250
RRRR	R250–300
RRRRR	over R300

Grand Provence Restaurant

🔟 Restaurants Around Franschhoek

1 The Tasting Room at Le Quartier Français

Among the world's 50 best restaurants, patrons of the Tasting Room are served five- or eight-course menus. ✆ *Map F2 • 16 Huguenot Rd • 021 876 8442 • Closed for lunch. Dinner only by reservation • RRRRR*

2 Reuben's Restaurant and Bar

Named after owner and chef Reuben Riffel, this award-winner has an innovative menu with African, Asian and European influences. ✆ *Map F2 • 19 Huguenot St • 021 876 3772 • RRRRR*

3 Fyndraai

Known for its modern take on traditional Cape cuisine, the menu explores the culinary heritage in a historic atmosphere. ✆ *Map F2 • Solms-Delta Wine Estate, off R45, Groot Drakenstein • 021 874 3937 • RRRRR*

4 Grande Provence Restaurant

Set on the estate of the same name, this upmarket restaurant serves a highly recommended à la carte menu, with a six-course wine pairing by arrangement. ✆ *Map F2 • Main Rd • 021 876 8600 • RRRRR*

5 Haute Cabrière Cellar Restaurant

Offering stunning views from a 17th-century estate, this restaurant serves French/South African contemporary dishes. ✆ *Map F2 • Pass Rd • 021 876 3688 • RRRRR*

6 La Petite Ferme

With a glass veranda offering views over the Franschhoek Valley, this restaurant is one of the Winelands' loveliest. The global menu does the location full justice. ✆ *Map F2 • Pass Rd • 021 876 3016 • RRRR*

7 Mange Tout Restaurant

This fine dining restaurant in the Mont Rochelle Hotel is notable for its contemporary continental cuisine. ✆ *Map F2 • Mont Rochelle, Dassenberg Rd, Franschhoek • 021 876 2770 • RRRRR*

8 Pierneef à la Motte

La Motte's gallery of Pierneef artworks inspired the name of the restaurant and their certified organic wines. Ancient recipes, historically researched, result in high quality authentic cuisine *(see p88)*.

9 Bread & Wine

With the same management as Le Quartier Français *(see p116)*, this family-oriented lunch venue on the Môreson Estate serves sumptuous charcuterie and inventive country cuisine. ✆ *Map F2 • Môreson Farm • 021 876 3692 • Lunch only • RR*

10 Boschendal Wine Estate

This estate has three lunch options – a buffet restaurant in the manor house, a cheerful café and French-style picnic baskets. ✆ *Map E2 • Pniel Rd, Groot Drakenstein • 021 870 4274 • Café: RR, picnic: RR, restaurant: RRR*

As a rule, restaurants on wine estates are open for lunch only, while those in town serve dinner too.

Skilpad Wildflower Reserve in Namaqualand

Beyond the Winelands

ASSUMING YOU CAN DRAG YOURSELF *away from its estimable charms,
Cape Town provides a great base for exploring the rest of the Western
Cape, a province notable for its consistently scenic coastline, fynbos-swathed
mountains and ever-expanding viniculture industry. Highlights east of Cape
Town include the peerless, land-based whale watching in Walker Bay and the
underrated De Hoop Nature Reserve – not to mention Agulhas, the most
southerly tip of Africa – while the west coast stretching up towards Lamberts
Bay combines ruggedly beautiful seaside scenery with some of the world's
most spectacular floral displays.*

Left **A fisherman's cottage at Paternoster** Right **Fishing trawlers in Lamberts Bay harbour**

Sights

1. Hermanus
2. Gansbaai
3. Agulhas National Park
4. De Hoop Nature Reserve
5. Swellendam
6. Cederberg Conservancy
7. West Coast National Park
8. Paternoster and Cape Columbine
9. Lamberts Bay
10. Namaqualand

Preceding pages **Grapevines in Stellenbosch vineyards**

Hermanus

Southeast of Cape Town, the quaint small town of Hermanus is perched on the sheer cliffs that hem in Walker Bay. Its attractions include the montane *fynbos* of Fernkloof Nature Reserve. But above all, Hermanus is the world's best place for some land-based whale viewing from June to November. The movements of southern right whales, which regularly breach in the waters below town, are tracked by a "whale crier". ✆ *Map U5 • Tourist information: 028 312 2629 • www.hermanustourism.info*

Gansbaai

This fishing village, named after the geese that once nested here, is known for the sharks and whales that live offshore. Its shark safaris mostly focus on Dyer Island, which supports African penguins, black oystercatchers and the Cape fur seal colony. Nearby, the 2,000-year-old potshards unearthed at Klipgat Cave are among the oldest discovered in South Africa. ✆ *Map U6 • Tourist information: 028 384 1439 • www.gansbaaiinfo.com*

Agulhas National Park

The southernmost tip of Africa and meeting point of the Atlantic and Indian Oceans, Agulhas, named by Portuguese navigators, means "needles" – an allusion to the jagged offshore formations that have caused 250 shipwrecks. Home to South Africa's oldest lighthouse (built in 1849), its rocky beaches possess a stark charm. Proclaimed a national park in 1999, it has grown from just 4 ha to 21,000 ha. ✆ *Map V6 • 028 435 6078 • Open 9am–5pm daily • Adm for lighthouse • www.sanparks.co.za*

De Hoop Nature Reserve

To the east of Agulhas, this is South Africa's largest surviving coastal *fynbos* habitat. It is a breeding ground for the endemic bontebok and Cape mountain zebra. The coastline of tall dunes and sheer cliffs can be explored on short walking and mountain biking trails, or along a five-day hiking trail named after the whales that breach offshore between June and November. ✆ *Map W5 • 028 542 1253 • Open 7am–6pm daily • Adm • www.capenature.co.za*

Eland at the De Hoop Nature Reserve

The rocky coastline around Hermanus

Beyond the Winelands

Whales and Dolphins

A remarkable 42 species of whales and dolphins have been recorded in South African waters. The Western Cape is the prime whale spotting destination, thanks to the southern right whales that migrate to sheltered coves such as Walker and False Bays. Bottle-nosed dolphins are regularly seen here too, pirouetting in apparent glee as they follow a boat's wake.

Swellendam

Founded in 1745 at the Cape Colony's remote eastern frontier, this gracious small town has an old world atmosphere reinforced by Cape Dutch buildings such as the Old Drostdy (Magistrate's Seat), which was built in 1747 and is now a local history museum. Six kilometres (4 miles) out of town, a network of quiet roads and trails runs through the hilly *renosterveld* of Bontebok National Park, which was established in 1931 to protect the 30 last remaining wild bontebok, whose population has now risen to 200. ✆ *Map W5*
• *Swellendam Tourism: 028 514 2770*
• *www.swellendamtourism.co.za*

The Wolfberg Arch in Cederberg

Cederberg

The Cederberg Wilderness (Provincial Reserve) and the Cederberg Conservancy (private farmland) form the heart of Cederberg. The montane wilderness is revered in hiking circles for its stunning sandstone formations, such as the Wolfberg Arch and Maltese Cross, its profusion of prehistoric rock art and a rich endemic flora and fauna. Though best explored over several days, the conservancy also offers shorter day hikes in montane and karoo surroundings, with private camps providing access to rock art sites and views. ✆ *Map U2*
• *021 483 0190* • *www.capenature.co.za*

West Coast National Park

Extending around the sparkling waters of the Langebaan Lagoon, this pristine coastline lies just an hour's drive north of Cape Town. It is particularly worth visiting in August–September, when magnificent spring wildflowers bloom in the Postberg sector. Offshore islands support breeding colonies of ten different marine bird species. The recreational zone of the lagoon is popular with watersport enthusiasts. ✆ *Map S3* • *022 772 2144/5*
• *Open Apr–Sep 7am–7:30pm; Oct–Mar 6:30am–7:30pm; Postberg: open Aug & Sep only (flowering season) 9am–5pm*
• *Adm* • *www.sanparks.co.za*

Paternoster and Cape Columbine

The coastal village of Paternoster on Cape Columbine to the north of Cape Town is renowned for its traditional whitewashed fishermen's cottages and superb crayfish. The adjacent Columbine Nature Reserve protects a lovely stretch of coast that bursts into spectacular bloom from August to October and offers excellent

Renosterveld, a type of fynbos *found to the north of Cape Town, is dominated by the* renosterbos *(rhinoceros bush) shrub.*

White pelicans at Langebaan Lagoon

kayaking spots through the year. There is terrestrial and marine wildlife around too. ◈ Map S2

9 Lamberts Bay

The largest town on the west coast and famous for its crayfish, Lamberts Bay retains the feel of a sleepy port, and its pretty harbour is regularly visited by seals and other marine creatures. The main attraction is Bird Island (see p41) with its 20,000- to 30,000-strong colony of Cape gannets. Boat trips further afield come with a good chance of sighting the localized Heavyside's dolphin and other cetaceans. It is a good base for exploring the underrated Olifants River Wine Route. ◈ Map S1 • Lamberts Bay: 027 432 1000 • www.lambertsbay.co.za

10 Namaqualand

This desert to the north of Lamberts Bay hosts one of the world's most astonishing floral spectacles. Between August and September, its parched soils, soaked by light but predictable rains, transform the rocky plains into dazzling fields of multi-hued flowers, including some 300 species of daisy and other annuals. Ten per cent of the world's succulent species are endemic to the region, including surreal tree aloes such as the *kokerboom* (quiver tree) and bulbous *halfmensboom* (half human tree). ◈ Map T1 • 053 832 2657 • www.experiencenortherncape.com

Overnight Tour to Hermanus

Day 1

🕐 Follow the N2 east from Cape Town for 30 minutes, turning right onto the R44 at Strand. **Hermanus** (see p95) is 75 km (47 miles) from Strand, so you could make it in an hour, but it's worth stopping to admire the scenery. Rooiels Bay and Kleinmond offer wonderful views to **Cape Point** (see p36). **Harold Porter Botanical Garden** (see p98) in Betty's Bay is a great place to relax in a *fynbos* habitat. In Hermanus, check into a hotel and then lunch at the **Burgundy Restaurant** or grab a bite at beachfront **Dutchies** (see p99). In the afternoon, follow the Cliff Path west out of town. Or stroll around town keeping an eye out for whales, or in calm weather, head to **Onrus Beach**. End with dinner at the **Burgundy** or **The Marine Hermanus** (see p118).

Day 2

After an early breakfast, drive to **Gansbaai** (see p95) for a cruise to **Dyer Island** (see p95) to spot whales, dolphins and the fearsome great white shark. Alternatively, stay back and take a 2-hour boat-based whale cruise, or explore the town's boutiques. If at **Gansbaai**, lunch at the trendy **Great White House** (see p99). Then, if time permits, follow the longer route that connects with the N2 at Botrivier and runs west through Vredendal and Sir Lowry's Passes to **Somerset West** (see p98). A detour to **Vergelegen Wine Estate** (see p85) in the **Helderberg Mountains** is strongly recommended.

Left **A church in the town of Robertson** Right **Harold Porter National Botanical Garden**

⁞O Best of the Rest

1 Strand
Situated 50 km (30 miles) from Cape Town, this resort town is named after the beach along its seaboard. ⊗ *Map D4 • 021 853 1688 • www.capetown.travel*

2 Harold Porter National Botanical Garden
This garden is dedicated to *fynbos* flora. ⊗ *Map E6 • Betty's Bay • 028 272 9311 • www.sanbi.org*

3 Kogelberg Biosphere Reserve
This reserve protects a *fynbos* habitat geared towards hiking, mountain biking and kayaking. ⊗ *Map E5 • 021 271 5138 • Open 7:30am–4pm daily • Adm • www.capenature.co.za*

4 Salmonsdam Nature Reserve
At the base of the Perdeberg Mountains, this reserve is crossed by day trails through montane *fynbos*. ⊗ *Map V5 • 028 341 0018 • Adm • www.capenature.co.za*

5 Robertson
Robertson lies along the Breede River wine route, whose estates offer better value than their counterparts around Stellenbosch and Franschhoek. ⊗ *Map V4 • www.robertsonr62.com*

6 Ceres
Named after the Roman goddess of agriculture, Ceres lies in the main centre of deciduous fruit production. ⊗ *Map U3 • www.ceres.org.za*

7 Karoo Desert National Botanical Garden
A largely uncultivated garden, known for its amazing displays of arid and semi-arid southern African plants. ⊗ *Map U4 • Roux Rd, Worcester • 023 347 0785 • Open 7am–7pm daily • Free except Aug–Oct • www.sanbi.org*

8 Melkbosstrand
A holiday spot north of Cape Town, popular with anglers, with a fine beach that offers views across Table Bay. ⊗ *Map T4*

9 Darling
This once-quaint town's Victorian railway station is now the venue for the risqué cabaret, Evita se Perron *(see p67)*. ⊗ *Map T3 • www.darlingtourism.co.za*

10 Rocherpan Nature Reserve
The bird species known from this seasonal wetland include the great white pelican and the great crested grebe. ⊗ *Map S2 • 082 319 1646 • Open May–Aug 8am–5pm daily • Adm • www.capenature.co.za*

➜ *For more information about* fynbos *flora,* **see pp76–9.**

Price Categories

For a three-course meal for one, including half a bottle of wine, cover charge, taxes and extra charges.

R	under R150
RR	R150–200
RRR	R200–250
RRRR	R250–300
RRRRR	over R300

Agulhas Country Lodge

🔟 Lunch Stops

1 Seafood at the Marine
This restaurant, in the five-star Marine Hermanus, is an excellent bet for a seafood lunch best enjoyed with the great wine list and a view of the legendary whales in the Walker Bay waters. ◈ Map U5 • Marine Dr, Hermanus • 028 313 1000 • RRRR

2 Dutchies
Their cosmopolitan food is enhanced by the attractive beach-front location. A great spot for watching whales. ◈ Map U5 • Grotto Beach, Hermanus • 028 314 1392 • RRR

3 Burgundy Restaurant
This seaview restaurant has a sophisticated menu with influences from the north and south of the Mediterranean. It is in one of the oldest buildings in Hermanus, which is now a heritage site. ◈ Map U5 • Marine Dr, Hermanus • 028 312 2800 • RRRR

4 Grootbos Forest Lodge
Drop into this lodge's restaurant for lunch or dinner in beautiful surroundings. Huge picture windows frame the view down towards the coastline. ◈ Map U6 • Grootbos Private Nature Reserve, R43, 13km past Stanford • 028 384 8000 • RRRRR

5 Agulhas Country Lodge
This hillside lodge is the pick of a somewhat limited choice of eateries in Agulhas. Excellent seafood and wine along with sublime views over Africa's most southerly point are the main draws. ◈ Map U6 • 673 Main Rd L'Agulhas • 028 435 7650 • RRRR

6 Tolhuis Bistro
Now a national monument, the former toll house at Mitchell's Pass is known for its steaks. It also offers country fare and light lunches. ◈ Map U3 • Ceres • 023 312 1211 • RR

7 Geelbek Restaurant
Located in a Cape Dutch house, Geelbek Restaurant specializes in South African fare, and has a reasonable vegetarian selection. ◈ Map S3 • West Coast National Park • 022 772 2134 • RRR

8 Marianas
Savour authentic country cooking. Mariana puts her passion into the food – using home-grown ingredients – while husband Peter explains each dish. Booking is advisable. ◈ Map U6 • 12 Du Toit St, Stanford • 028 341 0272 • Open lunch Thu–Sun • No credit cards • RRR

9 Die Strandloper
This eatery offers a tasty fish barbecue buffet. ◈ Map S3 • Langebaan Lagoon • 022 772 2490 • www.strandloper.com • Booking essential • No credit cards • RRRR

10 Muisbosskerm Restaurant
Linger over the buffet of Cape dishes at this restaurant on the beachfront. ◈ Map S1 • 5 km south of Lamberts Bay • 027 432 1017 • www.muisbosskerm.co.za • RRRR

Following pages Miniature ethnic masks, Greenmarket Square

STREETSMART

CAPE TOWN & THE WINELANDS' TOP 10

Left **Parliament House exterior** Centre **English and Afrikaans signage** Right **Electrical plugs**

TOP 10 General Information

1 Government

South Africa has been a multi-party democracy with an independent judiciary since May 1994. The Parliament, situated in Cape Town, comprises a representative National Assembly and National Council of Provinces. The dominant party since 1994 has been the African National Congress (ANC). The official opposition is the Democratic Alliance. Jacob Zuma, leader of the ANC, became president in May 2009.

2 Economy

South Africa has Africa's strongest economy and accounts for half the continent's mineral and industrial output. Cape Town is one of four main economic hotspots and the national leader in the tourist sector. Its average growth of 3–4 per cent since 1999 has been somewhat tempered in recent times.

3 Languages

South Africa has 11 official languages: Afrikaans, English, isiNdebele, isiXhosa, isiZulu, Sepedi, Sesotho, Setswana, siSwati, Tshivenda and Xitsonga. The most widely spoken language in the Cape Town area is English, followed by Afrikaans and isiXhosa. English is sufficient for almost all practical purposes.

4 Religions

Though there is freedom of worship, Christianity is dominant, with Zionist, Catholic, Methodist, Dutch Reformed and Anglican being the most common. The remaining population follows Islam, Judaism, other religions or are atheists.

5 Electricity

Very rare, localized cuts are experienced in Cape Town. All hotel rooms take the British Standard earthed plug. Most have adaptors for the twin-pronged unearthed plugs used in continental Europe.

6 Opening Hours

Post offices and government offices are open 8:30am–4:30pm Monday to Friday. Post offices are also open on Saturdays 8:30–11:30am. Timings for sights like museums and wine estates vary greatly *(see also p108 and p111)*.

7 Time Zone

South Africa is one or two hours ahead of the UK, six hours ahead of Eastern Standard Time and eight hours behind Australian Standard Time.

8 Embassies

Diplomatic represent-ation is in Pretoria (Tshwane) in Gauteng Province. The UK, the USA and Germany have consulates in Cape Town.

9 Public Holidays

South Africa has 12 annual holidays from the global to the national: 1 Jan (New Year's Day), 21 March (Human Rights Day), Good Friday, Easter Monday, 27 April (Freedom Day), 1 May (Workers' Day), 16 June (Youth Day), 9 Aug (National Women's Day), 24 Sep (Heritage Day), 16 Dec (Day of Reconciliation), 25 Dec (Christmas) and 26 Dec (Day of Goodwill).

10 Further Reading

Tremendous literature by prominent novelists include works by André P. Brink, Achmat Dangor and Nobel Prize winners JM Coetzee and Nadine Gordimer. Anthony Sampson's *Mandela: The Authorised Biography* and Mandela's autobiography, *Long Walk to Freedom*, are popular non-fiction books. A range of field guides focusing on the country's mammals, reptiles, trees and flowers can be picked up in any bookshop in Cape Town.

Consulates

UK Consulate
• *021 405 2400*

US Consulate
• *021 702 7300*

German Consulate
• *021 405 3000*

Visitors are often confused by the fact that any public holiday due to fall on a Sunday is carried over to the following Monday.

Left **An Internet café** Centre **Tourist information sign** Right **Customs banner at the airport**

🔟 Planning Your Trip

1 Tourist Information

Cape Town Tourism is the official Visitor Services Organization, with 12 world-class information centres within the city. Visit them for information about reservation and other auxiliary services.
🕾 021 487 6800 • www. tourismcapetown.co.za

2 Internet Resources

Many websites are dedicated to travel in Cape Town, the most useful being the official tourist board (www. capetown.travel). The unofficial www.cape-town.org and the listings-oriented www.capetowntoday.co.za are also popular. For Winelands coverage, www. winelands.co.za is useful, while foodies are pointed to www.eatout.co.za and www.restaurants.co.za.

3 Maps

Tourist offices in Cape Town stock a good selection of free maps and you can pick up plans for smaller towns at tourist offices. For detailed maps, Map Studio has the best. 🕾 Map Studio: Wembley Square, Solan St, Gardens • 021 460 5400 • www.mapstudio.co.za

4 Passports and Visas

Your passport should not be due to expire within six months of your intended date of departure from South Africa. It must contain at least two unused pages for stamps. Visas are not required by nationals of EU countries, the USA, Canada, Australia and New Zealand, who are granted a free three-month temporary visitor's permit upon arrival. Citizens of most other countries require a visa.

5 Customs

No customs duty is charged on items imported temporarily for personal use. Otherwise duty-free restrictions are standard.

6 Insurance

Travel insurance is highly recommended; there is no public health service, which means that all medical bills of uninsured travellers will have to be paid from their own pockets.

7 When to Go

The summer months of October–March are the peak tourist season, when facilities tend to be pricier. Winter is more of a lottery, with periods of beautiful, mild weather interspersed by days of cold, drizzle and wind. Late August–September is perfect; not too crowded, balanced weather and wonderful spring wildflowers on display.

8 What to Wear

Weather tends to be warm to mild in summer, so choose your wardrobe accordingly, and add in a couple of sweaters just in case. The winters (May–September) are cold and wet, making a jacket essential. Skimpily-clad women may be subject to unwanted male attention, unless at a beach.

9 What to Pack

Arm yourself against the sun with sunblock and a hat, especially if you are coming from the northern winter. Carry binoculars to spot wildlife. Stock up on prescription drugs but there's no need to be over-prepared – anything you forget can be bought in Cape Town.

10 How Long to Stay

Anything less than a week for Cape Town and the Winelands would feel restrictively short. It is easily possible to spend two weeks holidaying in and around the city and stay busy.

Tourist Information Offices

Cape Town CBD
Map Q4 • The Pinnacle Building, Cnr Burg and Castle Sts • 021 487 6800

Stellenbosch
Map D2 • 36 Market St • 021 883 3584

The V&A Waterfront
Map Q2 • Clock Tower • 021 405 4500

Left **Cape Town International Airport** Right **A taxi in Cape Town**

🔟 Getting to Cape Town

1 Flights from the USA and Europe

The main gateway for international flights to South Africa is OR Tambo International Airport in Johannesburg. It is connected to Cape Town by numerous domestic flights. A number of operators also fly directly to Cape Town from North America or Europe, notably British Airways and South African Airways (SAA) (www.flysaa.com).

2 Flights from within Africa

SAA operates a network of direct flights to African capital cities. Most major African national carriers fly between their capital city and South Africa, with connections to Europe and North America. Flights from elsewhere in Africa land in Johannesburg from where Cape Town-bound travellers need to catch a domestic flight.

3 Domestic Flights

The arrival of smaller airlines has ensured that cheap flights are available between Cape Town and other cities. You can shop online for details on such carriers as Mango, Kulula, 1time and Safair (see p107).

4 Airports

The Cape Town International Airport flanks the N2 highway 20 km (13 miles) east of the city centre. It is one of the busiest airports in Africa

and has an extensive range of shops and restaurants. 📞 *021 937 1200 • www.airports.co.za*

5 Airport Hotels

With the isolated location of Cape Town International Airport on the Cape Flats, travellers arriving late or leaving early may elect to stay in the inexpensive but well-equipped 90-room Road Lodge, the only hotel adjacent to the airport. 📞 *Map C3 • 021 934 7303 • www.citylodge.co.za*

6 Leaving the Airport

MyCiTi (www.myciti.org. za) offers airport to city centre transfers every 20 minutes (4:55am–9:40pm) for around R70, and some hotels offer free airport transfers. Otherwise, Randy's operates a regular shuttle to and from the city centre, the V&A Waterfront, Green Point and Camps Bay starting at R350, depending on destination and group size. Private taxis are available at a higher price, as are several rental cars. 📞 *Randy's: 021 706 0166 • www.randystours.com*

7 Intercity Buses

Intercity buses con- nect Cape Town to Johannesburg, Pretoria, Port Elizabeth, Durban and Upington. The fares are inexpensive. Major opera- tors include Greyhound (www.grey hound.co.za),

Intercape (www.intercape. co.za), Translux (www. translux.co.za), and Intercity Xpress (www. intercity.co.za).

8 Self-Drive

Car rental rates start at R150 per day and include 200 km (125 miles) free usage. Most major international players are represented. International operators such as Avis (www.avis. co.za) and Hertz (www. hertz.co.za) are costlier than local companies such as AA Car Hire (www. aacarhire capetown.co.za) and Tempest Sixt (www. tempestcarhire.co.za).

9 Trains

Few tourists use passenger trains as they are not safe, but details are available at www. transnetfreightrail-tfr.net. Popular exceptions are the Blue Train between Pretoria or Johannesburg and Cape Town (www. bluetrain.co.za) and the luxurious trains of Rovos Rail (www.rovosrail.co.za).

10 Ocean Cruises

An unusual way to get to Cape Town is by one of the cruise ships that dock there en route to Indian Ocean Islands and Europe. Particularly legendary is the world's last operating mail ship, the *RMS St Helena* (www. rms-st-helena.com) run- ning annually between Southampton and St Helena.

Left **Filling station** Centre **Car rental agency** Right **Local bus on city roads**

TOP 10 Getting Around

1 Rikki Taxis
Fulfilling a function somewhere between normal cabs and African "shared taxis", these cabs can be booked by phone or hailed on the street through the city centre and select suburbs. There are "Rikki Phones" at various locations. They take up to five people and are far cheaper than bona fide taxis. ✆ 086 174 5547 • 24 hours daily • www.rikkis.co.za

2 Taxis
Taxis in the city are inexpensive by international standards at around R10/km. There are few roving taxis, but you can hire one at a taxi rank (Long St, outside most major upmarket hotels and malls) or ring an operator. ✆ Marine: 021 434 0434; Sea Point Taxis: 021 434 4444; Unicab: 021 448 1720

3 Car Rental
The Cape Peninsula and the Winelands are well suited to self-driving. The distances are quite small, so you should be alright within the free limit of 150–200 km (94–125 miles) that is imposed by most companies. Do be aware that the additional "per km" costs will build up quickly if you do something like drive between Johannesburg and Cape Town!

4 Filling Stations
Most filling stations stay open 24 hours and have decent shops attached. The price of fuel falls somewhere between fuel costs in Europe and the USA, and can be paid for with a credit or debit card. Some stations only accept a locally issued petrol card, so you'll need to pay cash.

5 Parking
Multi-storey car parks dot the city. Car parks are also attached to tourist attractions such as the Company's Garden and Castle of Good Hope. Most streets have an attendant who'll guard your car for a tip (R5–10).

6 Bicycles
Probably inadvisable in the city centre, cycling can be a very enjoyable way of getting around the sunny countryside, provided you're aware of the considerable distances between places. A recommended agency for bike rental is Downhill Adventures (021 422 0388, www.downhilladventures.com).

7 Walking
This is the cheapest – and healthiest – way of getting about and most major attractions in central Cape Town are within walking distance of each other. It is advisable to avoid wearing valuables. Take advice from locals about where to go after dark; avoid walking alone. If in doubt hail a taxi cab or a Rikki.

8 Buses
MyCiti bus terminals are dotted around the city, but the hub for metropolitan bus services is the Golden Acre Bus Terminal on Strand Street. The bus network is more limited in outlying suburbs. The open-top sightseeing buses are popular with tourists (see p107).

9 Trains
The main railway station is on Adderley Street. A great experience is the "hop-on, hop-off" ticket for the scenic southern line between Cape Town and Simon's Town (their detailed map highlights attractions near key stations). There's a regular service to Stellenbosch. ✆ 080 065 6463 • Ticket: R30–R50 • www.capemetrorail.co.za

10 Organized Excursions
Without private transport, organized excursions are the best way to get to remote places such as the Cape of Good Hope Nature Reserve (see p26). They are also the safest option to visit townships or to explore the Winelands. Hotels or tourist offices can recommend operators.

If you do plan to cycle around the Cape Peninsula, be aware that it is forbidden to carry bicycles on metropolitan trains.

Left **Ostrich on the road** Centre **A tube of sunscreen** Right **Cloud cover over Table Mountain**

🔟 Things to Avoid

1 Road Hazards
South Africans are known for their assertive driving style, and Capetonians are no exception. Be particularly cautious of the notoriously whimsical minibuses that serve as public transport. In the rural Winelands, be alert to the possibility of livestock suddenly crossing the road and drunken pedestrians weaving in front of your vehicle.

2 Sun
People who are unused to the ozone-depleted, cloudless southern sky are inclined to underestimate the strength of the sun here (see p109). Wear strong sunblock and a wide-brimmed hat whilst out walking, as well as on boat trips, when the reflection from the water intensifies the sun's rays.

3 Snakes
Although snakes are present on Table Mountain and in nature reserves, most species are harmless; even the venomous ones tend to flee when they sense the seismic vibration of an approaching human foot. The risk of snakebite can be further reduced by wearing solid shoes and trousers on nature trails. Also be sure that you avoid rummaging through woodpiles or picking up stones with gloveless hands.

4 Feeding Baboons
Baboons fed by people perceive them as a source of food, which can lead to aggressive confrontations. Deliberately feeding a baboon encourages this, and may eventually lead to it being shot. All the same, should one confront you over food, surrender the titbit immediately – the doglike incisors of a baboon can inflict a nasty bite.

5 HIV and AIDS
The rate of HIV infection in South Africa is very high. The most certain way to avoid infection is abstinence. Failing that, condoms can provide a high level of protection; these can be bought at pharmacies, supermarkets and convenience stores at filling stations.

6 ATM Scams
Two scams are associated with ATMs. One involves a helpful local making off with your card, while the other entails causing cards to get stuck mid-transaction. You are most vulnerable outside of banking hours and at remote locations. Never reveal your PIN to a stranger and ensure nobody can see it when you type it in.

7 Mugging
The odds of being mugged are small, provided that you follow common sense advice and exercise caution (see p109). In the unlikely event you are accosted, you're likely to walk away unscathed if you cooperate with your assailants.

8 Weather Changes on the Mountain
The fickle weather of Table Mountain claims a few lives every year. Don't even think about hiking on the mountain in stormy weather. Even on clear days, be alert to the possibility of changing conditions. Should mist suddenly descend, do the same – though if visibility is poor, it is best to wait for help.

9 Swimming in Dangerous Conditions
Although the occasional shark attack tends to grab headlines, a bigger danger to swimmers is riptides and other strong currents in stormy weather. Never swim without seeking local advice, in poor weather or where no other swimmers are present.

10 Drunk-Driving on Wine Routes
Driving after wine-tasting is potentially dangerous, and is illegal. Unless you have a designated driver who's prepared to abstain, join one of the inexpensive day tours operating out of Cape Town or Stellenbosch (see pp28–9).

Left **City sightseeing bus** Centre **Bringing your own wine** Right **Happy Hour cocktail**

🔟 Budget Tips

1 Cheap Domestic Flights

A boom in domestic carriers has led to wide availability of cheap air tickets – indeed, if you are flexible about dates, it may well be cheaper to fly between Johannesburg or Durban and Cape Town than to take a coach or train. For more information, try www.flymango.com, www.kulula.com and www.flysaa.com.

2 Off-Season Hotel Rates

As with any seasonal destination, Cape Town has a glut of empty rooms during the low season. Several hotels offer fantastic walk-in and last-minute online rates from May to September, sometimes as low as R300 for a double room (little more than a back-packer hostel). Check Protea and City Lodge chains for good deals. See www.citylodge.co.za and www.proteahotels.com for information.

3 Free Activities

Although entrance fees to Cape Town's main tourist attractions are generally reasonable, they quickly add up. You can save a packet by using free alternatives. Set a day aside to walk up Table Mountain rather than using the cableway or walk up Lion's Head, spend an afternoon feeding pigeons and watching squirrels in the Company's Garden or take a long stroll along Noordhoek Beach.

4 Happy Hour

Many bars in Cape Town have a Happy Hour, when drinks are half-price, or you get a second drink for the price of one. Ask around!

5 Mini-bus Taxis

Mini-buses generally operate along Victoria, Regent and Strand roads, and Long, Kloof and Buitenkant streets from early morning to evening. Shared taxis can be flagged down as one passes or while standing at a bus stop. Always ask where their final stop is before embarking. Tell the driver when you want to get off, and thank him or her when alighting. Fares range from R5 to R20.

6 City Sightseeing Buses

A popular, inexpensive way of getting around Cape Town is the open-topped hop-on, hop-off City Sightseeing Bus, which follows two routes – the Red Route and the Blue Route. It costs R150 for a day's unlimited usage. ✆ 021 511 6000 • www.citysightseeing.co.za

7 Cheap Day Tours

Cheap day tours are more convenient than public transport and are cheaper than taxis.

Tours offered by several companies include outings to Cape Point and Boulders, wine-tasting visits, township visits and adventure activities. You can book tours through the agencies along Long Street.

8 Bring Your Own Wine (Corkage)

Many restaurants allow diners to bring their own wine, which often saves on the price charged on the wine list, even where a corkage fee (typically R30–40 or more) is levied. Check ahead when you call in for a reservation.

9 Picnic and Self-Catering

Cape Town is studded with good supermarkets, and canny travellers can save a small fortune in restaurant bills by self-catering, or putting together picnic baskets. Excellent picnic spots include the Company's Garden, Boulders Beach, or wine estates around Stellenbosch.

10 Use Your Feet

The cheapest way to get around is, of course, on foot. The compact districts of Cape Town, Stellenbosch and Franschhoek all reward pedestrian exploration. Keen walkers could extend their rambling to include suburban wine estates such as Mont Rochelle or Lanzerac.

The hop-on, hop-off Baz Bus (www.bazbus.com) connects Johannesburg to Cape Town via Durban and the Garden Route.

Left **ATM** Centre **Post and courier service** Right **Local newspapers**

⅂⅊⅄⅃0 Banking and Communications

1 Currency
South Africa's currency is the rand, divided into 100 cents, locally denoted by the symbol R, and internationally by the prefix ZAR. Bank notes are in denominations of R10, R20, R50, R100 and R200. Coins come in denominations of R5, R2, R1, 50c, 20c, 10c and 5c.

2 Banking Hours
Most banks are open 9am–3:30pm Monday–Friday. City banks are open 8:30–11:30am on Saturday, but this may not be the case in small towns. Banks at international airports generally stay open late into the night.

3 Foreign Exchange
Most banks have foreign exchange facilities, and private bureaux de changes (locally called forex bureaux) are also found in malls and airports, typically keeping longer hours than banks. Most hotels also offer exchange facilities but at comparatively poor rates. All foreign exchange transactions are documented and you are required to show your passport. Exchange rates are non-negotiable and there is no black market.

4 Credit Cards
Major international credit and debit cards are accepted by practically all hotels, restaurants, shops and other outlets dealing with tourists. The most widely accepted card is Visa, followed by MasterCard. American Express is less widely used in South Africa, and may not always be accepted. You will be asked for "cheque" or "savings", which relates to local banking accounts. Market stalls and small enterprises expect cash.

5 ATMs
Most banks have at least one ATM where cash can be withdrawn using international cards, typically to a value of R1,000 (around US$100) per transaction. There are also ATMs in many airports and filling station shops. ATM-associated crime is common, so be careful when you withdraw money *(see p106)*.

6 Telephone
Local and international calls can be made from most phone booths and hotel rooms. Cape Town has a 021 prefix and the international code for South Africa is +27. Calls out of South Africa are prefixed by 00. Mobile (cell) phones are in wide use and numbers start with 07 or 08.

7 Internet
Internet cafés with broadband are dotted all over Cape Town and are generally quite cheap.

Most hotels also offer Internet facilities, but at inflated rates. Wi-Fi is available at international airports, cafés, restaurants and select hotels. If you need it, it is best to check if the hotel has the facility before you make a reservation.

8 Post, Shipping and Courier
International post in and out of South Africa is reliable but slow – airmail to Europe typically takes about a week and to North America at least two weeks. A faster service is offered by a private chain called PostNet, found in most large malls. Use an international courier such as FedEx or DHL for items of value.

9 Newspapers
Unlike during apartheid, South Africa now has freedom of press. Several English-language newspapers are available in Cape Town, notably the *Cape Argus*, *Cape Times*, *Sunday Times* and the *Mail & Guardian*.

10 Television
Public TV is restricted to three channels operated by state broadcaster SABC and privately run eTV. Both are heavy on American fare and loud advertising. Most hotels and sports bars have cable TV offering an array of movie, sports and international news.

Expect to use your mobile a lot in South Africa. You can save money by buying a local SIM card or renting a phone at airport kiosks.

Left **Sunblock is advised for sunbathers** Centre **Private medical service** Right **Policeman's badge**

🔟 Security and Health

1 Medical Insurance
Medical insurance is practically essential, as you'll be dependent on private healthcare facilities in the case of illness. Standards of private healthcare are high, and it is relatively cheap compared to the USA or Europe.

2 Vaccinations
Vaccinations advised for trips to most tropical countries aren't really applicable to the Cape Town area, though you should get polio or tetanus boosters if these have expired. No vaccination is mandatory for North Americans or Europeans, but anybody coming via a yellow fever area (anywhere else in Africa) might be asked to show a vaccination certificate at immigration.

3 Emergency Numbers
Nationwide emergency numbers are 10111 for the police and 10177 for ambulance (no area code required). Local emergency numbers will be listed in your hotel directory, though it is best to inquire at the reception before dialling.

4 Medical Facilities and Pharmacies
The Cape Town area is serviced by several hospitals that broadly conform to Western standards. Other facilities such as dentists and physiotherapists are also widely available – ask your hotel for a local recommendation. Most pharmacies keep standard business hours, but there are late-night and even 24-hour ones, including M-Kem on Durban Rd, Bellville (021 948 5706).

5 Malaria
Although malaria is present in South Africa, it is restricted to the north-ern and eastern border areas. There is no need to take precautions if your travels are restricted to the Western Cape, which is entirely malaria-free, but seek advice about prophylactic drugs if you plan on visiting Kruger Park or the coastal belt north of Durban.

6 Sunburn
Excessive exposure to the harsh sun is a perennial hazard for tourists hailing from gloomier climes. Overdo the sunbathing and you risk a painful sunburn or, in extreme cases, severe sunstroke. Dedicated sun-worshippers are advised to smother themselves in strong sunblock and to restrict tanning to one hour, preferably when the sun is low in the sky.

7 Drinking Water
You can assume that all tap water in Cape Town is safe to drink unless you have been specifically warned to the contrary. Bottled water is widely available for those who prefer it.

8 Public Toilets
Public toilets are generally maintained to Western standards, though facilities are occasionally on the grubby side. Most filling stations and shopping malls have well signposted toilets. In the city centre you may need to look a little harder – or ask nicely and slip into a restaurant or hotel.

9 Mugging and Crime
Avoid carrying large sums of cash, and having any cameras loose. Do not leave your belongings unattended. In general take advice from locals about where to go after dark (see p106). In parti-cular, take precautions at lonely lookout points, especially after dusk. Patrols and CCTV cameras offer more visible policing, but visitors should still remain vigilant.

10 Dangerous Wildlife
Snakes and scorpions present a small but real danger when walking in nature reserves, so counter the threat by wearing solid shoes and long trousers. Shark attacks occur sporadically in False Bay, often on surfers, but the risk can be reduced by avoiding swimming with an open wound or between dusk and dawn, when sharks are most active.

Left *Pink Map* guide Right Backpackers' accommodation

TOP 10 Special Concerns

Disabled Travellers
Though facilities for disabled travellers in South Africa are not very sophisticated, the situation is improving. Most hotels, malls and tourist sights have wheelchair access. The main paths at Kirstenbosch are wheelchair-friendly and also have a Braille Trail. Check www.eco-access. org for details of wheelchair accessibility at various other reserves countrywide. If you plan on renting a car, be sure to ask for a special parking disk that allows for parking concessions.

Special Needs Tour Operators
Several tour operators specialize in itineraries for disabled travellers. Flamingo Tours (www. flamingotours.co.za) and Endeavour Safaris (www. endeavour-safaris.com) are both experienced and offer itineraries catering to most disabilities. A recommended operator on a national level is Rolling South Africa (www.rollingsa.co.za).

Women Travellers
Attitudes towards women are less enlightened than in most Western nations, but many women travel alone in South Africa. However, dress conservatively in rural areas and be sure to avoid walking alone in lonely areas or after dark.

Backpackers
Cape Town is a backpackers' hotspot with several dozen hostels catering to budget travellers. It also offers an excellent selection of short and long tours, locally and further afield. The website www.coastingafrica. com is an invaluable resource for backpackers, as is the associated free booklet, *Coast To Coast*.

Camping
There are plenty of good campsites around Cape Town and in most nature reserves, usually with good washing facilities and cooking areas. It is a great way to experience this beautiful region, especially if you have wheels, but lugging around a tent and gear can be quite restrictive.

Students
Travellers under the age of 26 or registered students may obtain reduced rates at certain tourist attractions and on public transport upon production of a valid student card.

Travel with Children
Cape Town has plenty to offer kids of all ages. Most hotels give significant discounts to youngsters (or allow them to share their parents' room for free) and many restaurants have inexpensive menus for children. Entrance fees to the sights and attractions for kids are typically half to one-quarter of the adult fee.

Senior Travellers
Cape Town is a popular destination with senior travellers; facilities for seniors are better here than elsewhere in Africa. Substantial discounts on many services and activities are offered.

Gay and Lesbian Travellers
South Africa has an enlightened constitution when it comes to gay and lesbian rights. Cape Town is the main hub of the country's homosexual community and is recognized as a leading gay destination. Elsewhere in South Africa, however, on-the-ground attitudes tend to lag behind official policy; overt homosexual behaviour could attract unwanted trouble.

Gay Resources
The gay travel sites, www.capetown.tv and www.capeinfoafrica.co.za include information about gay-friendly guesthouses and facilities. A more hard-hitting source of gay news and views, www. capetownpride.org is also the official site of the Cape Town Pride Festival, taking place over February–March (see p54). The *Pink Map* is another good source of information.

For details on disabled facilities available, contact the Association for Persons with Disabilities at (021) 555 2881.

Left **The V&A Waterfront shopping centre** Centre **Self-catering accommodation** Right **Tipping**

Shopping, Eating and Hotel Tips

Shopping Hours
Shopping hours are usually 9am–5pm Monday–Friday, but some outlets stay open until 6pm. Stores in malls such as Victoria Wharf (The V&A Waterfront) stay open until 9pm. Shops that are open on weekends have shorter trading hours.

VAT Refunds
Non-resident foreign passport holders on a visit to South Africa can claim a VAT refund of 14 per cent on all purchases over R250 intended for export. This is best done before leaving; it involves presenting all invoices to VAT refund offices at Cape Town International Airport or the OR Tambo International Airport in Johannesburg. ✪ *Vat Refund: Clock Tower Bldg, The V&A Waterfront • Open 9am–5pm Mon–Sat, 10am–5pm Sun.*

Crafts and Curios
Cape Town is a great place to buy crafts from around Africa, with markets and shops at the V&A Waterfront, on Long Street at Hout Bay's fishing harbour and on the main road through Kalk Bay.

Breakfasts
Most smart hotels include breakfast in the room rate. Typically, this will be an extensive buffet of hot and cold dishes that sets you up for the day. Where it isn't included in the room rate, you'll be better off grabbing a hot drink and croissant at one of the delicatessens and coffee shops scattered around. Kloof Street is a good place for cheap breakfasts.

Lunches
When out sight-seeing, you can grab a bite to eat at any of the eateries that are attached to most of the tourist attractions. On more leisurely summer days, a lingering seafood lunch at the Waterfront is highly recommended, ideally accompanied by a bottle of crisp white wine.

Dinners
For most locals, dinner is the main meal of the day. If you eat out, it is usually a three-course affair. Money-conscious tourists should note that starters and desserts tend to push up the price of a meal, and a well-chosen main course should suffice. In summer, it is pleasant to eat dinner alfresco, but this isn't realistic over May–September.

Picnicking
A popular lunchtime option on the Wine Route is to picnic on the lawn of your chosen estate – Boschendal and Spier in particular provide excellent picnic baskets, as does the Moyo Kirstenbosch restaurant. You can also put together a picnic lunch at a supermarket.

Tipping
Waiters and bar staff tend to be paid very poorly and depend on tips, which should be in the 10–15 per cent range depending on the quality of service. Give cash rather than adding the tip to your bill and paying by card. It is customary to tip hotel porters around R2–5 per bag. Elsewhere, tips are discretionary.

Self-Catering Accommodation
Opting for self-catering accommodation can save you from running up high restaurant bills and also offers greater freedom of choice. For self-catering properties in and around Cape Town, try Cape Letting (www.capeletting. com) and Afribode Accommodation (www. afribode.com). Most backpacker hostels offer self-catering facilities.

Seasonal Discounts
The low season (May–September) is a good time for last-minute deals. Check websites of chains such as Protea and City Lodge and you may find three-star hotel rooms going for as little as R400–500. If you can't find a good deal online, book into a hotel for your first night and look for cheaper walk-in options once you are there.

Left **Twelve Apostles Hotel & Spa** Right **The Grand Daddy**

Upmarket Hotels

1 Mount Nelson Hotel

With its timeless and iconic Victorian exteriors, elegant rooms, a fine dining restaurant and grand views, the "Nellie" is the city's most prestigious hotel. The afternoon teas served with obsequious gravity on the patio are highly recommended. ✪ Map P6 • 76 Orange St • 021 483 1000 • www.mountnelson. co.za • RRRRR

2 One&Only Cape Town

An urban resort with contemporary African flair in the heart of fashionable Victoria & Alfred Waterfront. It has 131 rooms and suites, 40 of them on an island. ✪ Map P2 • Dock Rd, V&A Waterfront • 021 431 5888 • capetown.oneand onlyresorts.com • RRRRR

3 Derwent House

This boutique hotel, located in the heart of the City Bowl, has rooms with views of Table Mountain. The stylish decor is complemented by excellent facilities, including a large deck, solar-heated pool and hot tub. ✪ Map M6 • 14 Derwent Rd • 021 422 2763 • www.derwent house.co.za • RRRR

4 Cape Grace

The aptly named Cape Grace offers stylish accommodation, a mind-boggling array of services, tasty Cape fusion cuisine and an informal but attentive management. Some rooms have a private balcony. ✪ Map Q2 • West Quay Rd, The V&A Waterfront • 021 410 7100 • www.capegrace. com • RRRRR

5 Victoria & Alfred Hotel

Converted from a former Victorian warehouse, this hotel rises from the heart of the V&A Waterfront, ensuring that all the airy rooms have good views. Loft suites come with a heavier price tag than standard rooms. ✪ Map R3 • Pierhead • 021 419 6677 • www.newmark hotels.com • RRRRR

6 Westin Cape Town

This state-of-the-art hotel is a tower looming over the Waterfront. Geared mainly towards business travellers, it has a rather characterless feel, but there's no quibbling with the five-star facilities. ✪ Map Q3 • 1 Lower Long St • 021 412 9999 • www.westincapetown. com • RRRRR

7 Waterfront Village

This five-star all-suite accommodation offers luxury self-catering apartments with many amenities, making it suitable for families. ✪ Map Q2 • 4 West Quay Rd, The V&A Waterfront • 021 421 5040 • www. waterfrontvillage.com • RRRRR

8 The Grand Daddy Hotel

Without a doubt the most delightful feature of this creatively designed hotel is the penthouse trailer park on the roof. Featuring seven vintage Airstream caravans each uniquely decorated by local artists, such as the Goldilocks and the Three Bears caravan by Mark and Joe Stead. ✪ Map P5 • 38 Long Street • 021 424 7247 • www.granddaddy. co.za • RRRR

9 The Bay Hotel

This elegant hotel with its curvaceous exterior offers direct access to the popular Camps Bay beach. Well-equipped (as you would expect a five-star hotel to be), the hotel's upper-storey rooms offer stunning mountain views. ✪ Map H1 • 69 Victoria Rd, Camps Bay • 021 438 4444 • www.thebay.co.za • RRRRR

10 Twelve Apostles Hotel & Spa

Located on the edge of the Atlantic Ocean and at the foot of the Twelve Apostles formation, this five-star boutique hotel has exceptional rooms, superb service and an outstanding spa. It also offers guided walks and picnics into the surrounding fynbos. ✪ Map H1 • Victoria Rd, Camps Bay • 021 437 9255 • www.12apostleshotel. com • RRRRR

Unless otherwise stated, all hotels accept credit cards, have en-suite bathrooms and air conditioning.

Price Categories		
For a standard, double room per night (breakfast not included), taxes and services charges.	**R** under R500	
	RR R500–1,000	
	RRR R1,000–1,500	
	RRRR R1,500–2,000	
	RRRRR over R2,000	

Left **Cape Town Hollow Boutique Hotel** Right **Cape Heritage Hotel room**

🔟 Mid-Range Hotels

1 Cape Town Hollow Boutique Hotel

This contemporary four-star hotel is within walking distance of plenty of restaurants, bars and nightspots. It has an Italian restaurant and a spa. 🗺 *Map P5 • 88 Queen Victoria St • 021 421 5140 • www.seasonsinafrica.com/hotels-in-south-africa • RRR*

2 Cape Heritage Hotel

This historic hotel overlooking Heritage Square has 17 individually decorated rooms with antique features such as 19th-century wood floors and high-beamed ceilings. South Africa's oldest vineyard is in the courtyard. 🗺 *Map Q4 • 90 Bree St • 021 424 4646 • www.capeheritage.co.za • RRRR*

3 Cape Diamond Hotel

Overlooking the Company's Garden, this attractive relic of the 1930s Art Deco movement is wonderfully central and offers good value. Its ground-floor restaurant opens onto the street. 🗺 *Map Q5 • Cnr Longmarket & Parliament St • 021 461 2519 • Breakfast excluded • www.african skyhotels.com • RR*

4 Cape Milner

This chic city hotel has 57 rooms decorated with flair but not fuss in a refreshingly minimalist style. Services include Wi-Fi, 24-hour room service, a swimming pool and gym. 🗺 *Map N5 • 2a Milner Rd, Tamboerskloof • 021 426 1101 • www.capemilner.com • RRRR*

5 Four Rosmead Boutique Guesthouse

Built in 1903, this hotel is a classified monument that has been stylishly remodelled. The interiors are subtle but have a distinctive African spirit, enhanced by local art. Facilities include a pamper room and a patio overlooking a pool. 🗺 *Map N6 • 4 Rosmead Avenue, Oranjezicht • 021 480 3810 • www.fourrosmead.com • RRRR*

6 Winchester Mansions Hotel

This 1920s building set around a bougainvillea-clad courtyard has a beachfront location at Sea Point. Rooms on the lower floor have a floral Edwardian feel while those on the upper floors are spacious and contemporary. 🗺 *Map L2 • 221 Beach Rd, Sea Pt • 021 434 2351 • www.winchester.co.za • RRRR*

7 Peninsula All-Suite Hotel

This seafront Art Deco high-rise hotel offers spectacular views and has self-catering apartments. Facilities include a pool, a sunset deck and also a complimentary shuttle to various sites. The surrounding area has many shops for self-caterers. Popular with families and small groups. 🗺 *Map I4 • 313 Beach Rd, Sea Pt • 021 430 7777 • www.peninsula.co.za • RRRRR*

8 Wilton Manor

Lying in a quiet corner of Green Point, minutes away from the city centre, this restored Victorian manor has a wraparound balcony, pressed ceilings and wooden floors. Its thatched wooden deck has a heated pool. The seven double rooms can be booked individually or as a unit. 🗺 *Map N2 • 15 Croxteth Rd, Green Pt • 021 434 7869 • www.wilton guesthouses.co.za • RRR*

9 Cape Standard

Small and reasonably priced, this hotel combines modern European minimalism with subtle African touches to create a light, spacious feel and is within striking distance of the city centre. Its small, leafy garden has a plunge pool. 🗺 *Map M2 • 3 Romney Rd, Green Pt • 021 430 3060 • www.capestandard.co.za • RRR*

10 Three Boutique

Historic and modern combine in this boutique hotel housed in a building dating back to 1740. Relax in the black and white tiled wrap-around veranda or the pool terrace. 🗺 *Map P6 • 3 Flower St, Oranjezicht • 021 465 7517 • www.thethree.co.za • RRRR*

Left **Daddy Long Legs' "Doctor and Nurses" room** Centre **Protea Hotel** Right **Tudor Hotel**

TOP 10 Budget Hotels

1 Daddy Long Legs
Situated at the heart of the action on Long Street, this bold boutique hotel defies conventional description. Each of its 13 rooms have been uniquely, if rather bizarrely, decorated by different artists. ✆ *Map D4 • 134 Long St • 021 422 3074 • www. daddylonglegs.co.za • RR*

2 Protea Hotel Fire and Ice
This offshoot of the Protea chain is aimed at the younger, hipper crowd, with its action-themed decor, state-of-the-art viewing room and designer burger bar with views of the koi fish pond. Its 201 rooms are comfortable, but a touch cramped. ✆ *Map N5 • New Church St • 021 488 2555 • www.proteahotels. com • RRR*

3 Tudor Hotel
This three-star hotel – the oldest in the city centre – has a sense of history complemented by an appealing, contemporary decor and good facilities. Each room is uniquely furnished. It is one of the best deals in central Cape Town. ✆ *Map P4 • 153 Longmarket St • 021 424 1335 • www. tudorhotel.co.za • RR*

4 Underberg Guest House
Built as a farmhouse in the 1860s, this charming 9-room guesthouse has a pretty setting below Table Mountain. Modern facilities include wireless connectivity. Its location is convenient to explore the city centre and the Waterfront. ✆ *Map N5 • 6 Tamboerskloof Rd, Tamboerskloof • 021 426 2262 • www.underberg guesthouse.co.za • RRR*

5 Holiday Inn Express
Stay in the heart of the city – within easy reach of all the tourist spots – at a reliable hotel chain, where you know what to expect. Compact rooms, but breakfast is included. ✆ *Map P4 • 101 St George's Mall, cnr of Church St • 021 480 8300 • www.hiexpress.com • RR*

6 V&A Waterfront City Lodge
Part of the national City Lodge chain, this hotel is an affordable option within walking distance of the Waterfront. Room rates are on par with the Breakwater, but the location is less convenient. ✆ *Map Q3 • Cnr Alfred & Dock Rds • 021 419 9450 • Breakfast excl • www.citylodge.co.za • RRR*

7 Protea Hotel Cape Castle
A few steps away from the V&A Waterfront, this hotel offers 65 suites with fully equipped kitchens, ranging from basic studio suites with mountain views, to superior luxury apartments with waterfront views. ✆ *Map P2 • 3 Main Rd, Green Point • 021 439 1016 • Breakfast excl • www. proteahotels.com • RR*

8 De Waterkant Village
This street-long complex in the Bo-Kaap area has 30 self-catering units, from simple crash pads to the more expensive plush apartments. It is perfect for visits to the boutiques, restaurants and nightclubs of De Waterkant (the Water's Edge). ✆ *Map P3 • 137 Waterkant St, De Waterkant • 021 437 9706 • www. dewaterkant.com • RRR*

9 Cape Town Ritz Hotel
Famous for its iconic revolving restaurant on the 21st floor, this hotel has modern rooms with superb views of the ocean and mountains. ✆ *Map L2 • Cnr Main & Camberwell Rds, Sea Pt • 021 439 6010 • www. africanskyhotels.com • RRR*

10 Road Lodge Cape Town International Airport
The only accommodation close to the international airport, this no-frills hotel is within walking distance of all terminals and offers cheap transfers to travellers with heavy luggage (see p104). ✆ *Map C3 • Cape Town International Airport • 021 934 7303 • www.citylodge.co.za • RR*

Price Categories

For a standard, double room per night (breakfast not included), taxes and service charges.

R	under R500
RR	R500–1,000
RRR	R1,000–1,500
RRRR	R1,500–2,000
RRRRR	over R2,000

Steenberg Hotel

Southern Suburbs & Peninsula Hotels

1 The Andros Boutique Hotel

One of the most exclusive addresses in Cape Town, this century-old Cape Dutch homestead was designed by Sir Herbert Baker. All eight rooms have verandas and antique furnishings. There is also a suite with a private pool. Facilities include a gym, beauty salon and a candle-lit country restaurant with French influences. ◈ *Map H2 • Cnr Newlands & Phyllis, Claremont • 021 797 9777 • www.andros. co.za • RRRRR*

2 Vineyard Hotel & Spa

Centred on a 200-year-old residence built for Lady Anne Barnard, this luxurious hotel offers a variety of accommodations, a quartet of restaurants that includes a sushi bar and a heated pool. ◈ *Map H2 • 60 Colinton Rd, Newlands • 021 657 4500 • www.vineyard.co.za • RRRRR*

3 Cellars-Hohenort

This gracious five-star hotel is set in grounds bordering Kirstenbosch National Botanical Garden. A classy set-up, it has a strong period feel and two excellent restaurants, of which the Cape Malay Experience *(see p52)* offers delicious Cape cuisine. ◈ *Map H2 • 93 Brommersvlei Rd, Constantia • 021 794 2137 • www.cellars-hohenort. com • RRRRR*

4 Constantia Uitsig

In the Constantia Winelands, this 16-room boutique hotel is built around a Cape Dutch farmhouse. Dine at the estate's three award-winning restaurants. ◈ *Map H2 • Spaanschemat River Rd, Constantia • 021 794 6500 • www.constantia-uitsig.com • RRRRR*

5 The Last Word Constantia

This boutique hotel has four superior doubles, and five suites. The hotel operates as a B&B combining contemporary decor with a scattering of modern African art. The staff prepares meals on request or you can explore the dining options nearby. ◈ *Map H2 • Spaanschemat River Rd, Constantia • 021 794 6561 • www.thelastword.co.za • RRRRR*

6 Steenberg Hotel

This intimate five-star hotel on the Steenberg Estate boasts fine thatched and gabled Cape Dutch architecture. The acclaimed Catharina's is also here *(see p75)*. Guests can access the exclusive Steenberg Golf Course. ◈ *Map H2 • Steenberg Estate, Tokai • 021 713 2222 • www.steenberg hotel.com • RRRRR*

7 Quayside Hotel

This wallet-friendly four-star hotel is wonderfully located in Quayside Centre. Its rooms are very large; it is worth paying the slight premium for a sea-facing one with a balcony. ◈ *Map H4 • Jubilee Sq, St George's St, Simon's Town • 021 786 3838 • http://quayside.ahagroup. co.za • RRR*

8 Monkey Valley Beach Nature Resort

A picture-perfect spot with self-catering cottages tucked into an indigenous milkwood forest over-looking a beach. It has a bar, restaurant and terrace. ◈ *Map G3 • Mountain Rd, off Beach Rd, Noordhoek • 021 789 8000 • www. monkeyvalleyresort.com • RRR*

9 Chartfield Guest House

This grand old building with 16 modern rooms overlooks Kalk Bay harbour. Shops, a beach and a glut of great restaurants are nearby. ◈ *Map H3 • 30 Gatesville Rd, Kalk Bay • 021 788 3793 • www.chartfield.co.za • RR*

10 Boulders Beach Lodge and Restaurant

In a beautiful location at the entrance to Boulders coastal park and penguin colony, this 14-room lodge (two self-catering) also has a restaurant. ◈ *Map H4 • 4 Boulders Plc • 021 786 1758 • www.bouldersbeach lodge.com • RR*

Left **Lobby of Oude Werf** Centre **Mont Rochelle** Right **Wild Mushroom Boutique Hotel**

Winelands Town Hotels

1 Oude Werf
Established in 1802 on the foundations of a fire-damaged church, this Stellenbosch institution is South Africa's oldest country inn. It has a handy location on historic Church Street. Atmospheric and affordable, it has well-equipped rooms and a fine Cape restaurant. Map D2 • 30 Church St, Stellenbosch • 021 887 4608 • www.oudewerf hotel.co.za • RRRR

2 Eendracht Hotel
An award-winning three-star village hotel set in a restored 18th-century homestead. Most of its dozen rooms come with private balconies that overlook historic Dorp Street. There's also a saltwater pool, a coffee shop and free Internet. Map D2 • 161 Dorp St, Stellenbosch • 021 883 8843 • www.eendracht-hotel.com • RRR

3 Protea Hotel Dorpshuis & Spa
This homely four-star boutique hotel is housed at the quieter end of historic Dorp Street. Antique furnishings decorate the 28 rooms, and there's a pool in the shady garden. Map D2 • 22 Dorp St, Stellenbosch • 021 883 9881 • www.proteahotels.com • RRRR

4 Batavia Boutique Hotel
Experience the grandeur of a classical 19th-century guesthouse with all the modern conveniences. The nine luxuriously appointed suites are individually designed with carefully selected antique and contemporary pieces. Map D2 • 12 Louw St, Stellenbosch • 021 887 2914 • www.bataviahouse.co.za • RRRR

5 Wild Mushroom Boutique Hotel
This luxurious boutique hotel has six suites, each one themed to a different mushroom species in an imaginative and sophisticated way. There is also a delightful garden and a swimming pool. Map D2 • 39 Digteby Estate, Vlottenburg Rd, Stellenbosch • 021 881 3586 • www.wildmush room.co.za • RRRR

6 Old Tulbagh Hotel
This small, family-run hotel stands in the historic heart of Tulbagh. Its spacious rooms have wooden floors and elegant furnishings. The attached Lounge Bar is a friendly pub that is popular with tourists and locals. Map H3 • 22 van der Stel Street, Tulbagh • 023 230 0071 • www.tulbaghhotel.co.za • RR

7 Le Quartier Français
Best known for its acclaimed restaurants, The Tasting Room and Bread & Wine, this legendary hotel offers five-star accommodation. Its large, hardwood-furnished rooms are situated around a leafy courtyard, a pool and a lounge bar. Map F2 • Berg & Wilhelmina Sts, Franschhoek • 021 876 2151 • www.lqf.co.za • RRRRR

8 Mont Rochelle
Previously known as Hotel Le Couronne, this five-star hotel on Mont Rochelle Wine Estate has wonderful views over Franschhoek. Built in the classic Cape Dutch style, it has elegant rooms and suites. It also has a wine-tasting centre. Map F2 • Dassenberg Rd, Franschhoek • 021 876 2770 • www.montrochelle.co.za • RRRRR

9 The Light House
It is five-star all the way at this boutique guesthouse, with sumptuous decor and just five large suites overlooking the expansive gardens and pool. Map E1 • 2 Lille St, Courtrai, Paarl • 021 873 4600 • RRRR

10 Grande Roche
One of the top hotels in the Winelands, Grande Roche on Paarl's outskirts is built around a lovely Cape Dutch manor now listed as a national monument. Its 34 plush suites come with wonderful views. Map E1 • Plantasie St, Paarl • 021 863 5100 • www.grande roche.com • RRRRR

Stellenbosch Lodge

TOP 10 Winelands Rural Hotels

1 Devon Valley
This popular, four-star country retreat on Sylvanvale Estate offers lovely views and retains an Edwardian feel. Enjoy walks through the surrounding vineyards. The hotel also boasts the award-winning Flavours Restaurant. ◈ *Map D2 • Devon Valley Rd, near Stellenbosch • 021 865 2012 • www.devon valleyhotel.com • RRRR*

2 Lanzerac
Situated on the outskirts of Stellenbosch, this prestigious hotel is centred on a handsome 300-year-old Cape Dutch estate. Equipped with five-star facilities, the whole set-up positively exudes luxury. ◈ *Map E3 • 1 Lanzerac Rd • 021 887 1132 • www.lanzerac.co.za • RRRRR*

3 Kleine Zalze Lodge
This lodge offers four-star accommodation (with the option for self-catering) close to Stellenbosch. It is set among oak trees with mountain and golf course views. Its Terroir restaurant is an acclaimed gourmet destination. ◈ *Map D3 • Strand Rd (off R44), Stellenbosch • 021 880 0740 • www.kleinezalze. co.za • RRRRR*

4 Stellenbosch Lodge
This four-star hotel is on the Blaauwklippen Estate, which is to the south of Stellenbosch. Its 53 functional rooms are in a Cape Dutch-styled thatch building. The hotel's restaurant specializes in traditional Cape cuisine. ◈ *Map D3 • Canterbury Lane, Blaauwklippen • 021 888 0100 • www.stblodge. co.za • RRRR*

5 Spier Hotel
This mould-breaking four-star hotel overlooks the Eerste River on Spier Farm, a short drive from Stellenbosch. Its bold decor is an adventurous fusion of African themes and modern art. Well placed to explore other estates. ◈ *Map D3 • Spier Wine Farm • 021 809 1100 • www.spier.co.za • RRRR*

6 Zevenwacht Country Inn
This cozy hilltop inn lies on Zevenwacht Estate and offers accommodation in air conditioned suites with private terraces; on a clear day, you can see as far as Table Bay. It has a clubhouse, pool, playground and an acclaimed restaurant. ◈ *Map C3 • Langverwacht Rd, Kuilsrivier • 021 900 5700 • www.zevenwacht. co.za • RRRR*

7 WedgeView Country House & Spa
Enjoy five-star luxury and the experience of a private country residence with individually decorated rooms, heated pools and a spa. Stunning views of the surrounding mountains and vineyards. ◈ *Map D3 • Bonniemile Rd, Stellenbosch • 021 881 3525 • www.wedgeview. co.za • RRRR*

8 Alluvia Specialist Winery Estate
Set on the eponymous boutique wine estate on Helshoogte Pass, this exclusive guesthouse consists of five stylishly decorated four-star suites and two self-catering five-star cottages. Wine-tasting is only for the guests (booking required for non-residents). Other activities include fly-fishing and golf. ◈ *Map E2 • Helshoogte Pass • 021 885 1661 • www.alluvia. co.za • RRRR*

9 Eikendal Lodge
This vine-draped lodge is set among the Eikendal Estate vineyards. There is a good restaurant and the facilities include a fly-fishing clinic. ◈ *Map D3 • R44 south of Stellenbosch • 021 855 3617 • www. eikendallodge.co.za • RRRR*

10 La Petite Ferme
The view over the entire Franschhoek wine valley from these suites and self-catering cottages is mesmerizing. There's a well-regarded restaurant and intimate winery, so you don't have to go far to eat and drink in style. ◈ *Map F2 • Franschhoek Pass Rd • 021 876 3016 • www.lapetiteferme. co.za • RRR*

Left **Farr Out Guesthouse** Centre **Cliff Lodge** Right **Agulhas Country Lodge**

⓾ Hotels Beyond the Winelands

1 The Marine Hermanus

The top address in Hermanus, offering accommodation in 40 rooms and suites. The patio is a natural vantage point for whale watching, and facilities include a spa, heated swimming pool, tidal pool, Internet lounge and two great restaurants. ✆ Map U5 • Marine Drive, Hermanus • 028 313 1000 • RRRRR

2 Misty Waves Boutique Hotel

This great set-up, a curvaceous double-storey building on the cliffs, has a lounge, pool, private Jacuzzis and a great seafood restaurant with stunning views across the bay, excellent for whale watching. ✆ Map U5 • 21 Marine Drive, Hermanus • 028 313 8460 • www.hermanusmisty beach.co.za • RRRRR

3 Abalone Guest Lodge

Situated on Sievers Point, this homely and pleasantly decorated guesthouse is well located for cliff walks, whale watching and exploring the small town centre. ✆ Map U5 • 306 Main Rd, Hermanus • 044 533 1345 • www. abalone lodge.co.za • RRR

4 Cliff Lodge

This award-winning guesthouse with a magnificent clifftop location outside Gansbaai offers grand views of Walker Bay. It consists of just four spacious rooms and a suite, a shared conservatory and deck with ocean views and a plunge pool. ✆ Map U6 • De Kelders, Gansbaai • 028 384 0983 • www. clifflodge.co.za • RRRR

5 Agulhas Country Lodge

Set on a hill overlooking the southernmost point in Africa, this family-run guesthouse offers just eight rooms, all with great views, and some of the best seafood on the south coast. ✆ Map V6 • Main Rd, L'Agulhas • 028 435 7650 • www.agulhas countrylodge.com • RRR

6 De Hoop Cottages and Lodges

A variety of Cape Dutch-style family cottages and smaller self-catering units are studded around this lovely reserve. It's all reasonably priced but take your own provisions, although there is a basic supply store and a restaurant. ✆ Map W5 • De Hoop Nature Reserve • 021 422 4522 • www. dehoopcollection.co.za • RR

7 Bushmanskloof Wilderness Reserve & Wellness Retreat

The rocky nature reserve setting resembles the Wild West, except for the zebra and antelopes dotting the plains. Excellent service, food and riverside cottages.

Nature drives included. ✆ Map U1 • R364, Cederberg Wilderness Area • 021 437 9278 • www.bush manskloof.co.za • RRRRR

8 Old Mac Daddy Luxury Trailer Park

Long, sleek Airstream trailers were imported from the USA to create part-caravan park, part-designer farm resort. Each one is artist-decorated in über-modern, sometimes outrageous themes. It's about a 1-hour drive east of Cape Town. ✆ Map F4 • Valley Rd, Elgin • 021 884 0241 • www.oldmacdaddy. co.za • RR

9 Farr Out Guesthouse

This pleasant four-room establishment on the outskirts of Paternoster also offers a rustic but plush wigwam tent in a fynbos field. It is a convenient place to enjoy the sights of Cape Columbine. ✆ Map S2 • 17 Seemeeusingel, Paternoster • 022 752 2222 • www. farrout.co.za • RR

10 Robertson Small Hotel

This grand Victorian building offers the smartest accommodation in town and has a fine in-house restaurant. The sleepy valley of wine and olives is a popular weekend escape from Cape Town. ✆ Map V4 • 58 Van Reenen St, Robertson • 023 626 720 • www.therobertson smallhotel.com • RRRR

Cat & Moose Backpackers

Price Categories

For a standard, double room per night (breakfast not included), taxes and services charges.

R	under R500
RR	R500–1,000
RRR	R1,000–1,500
RRRR	R1,500–2,000
RRRRR	over R2,000

Backpacker Hostels

1 Long Street Backpackers

The oldest, and probably the best, backpacker hostel along Long Street, this is within easy reach of the trendy nightspots. It is a secure, friendly and lively place for those who want to be at the heart of the urban action. ◎ Map P5 • 209 Long St • 021 423 0615 • Breakfast excl • www.longstreetback packers.co.za • R

2 Cat & Moose Backpackers

Another veteran of Long Street, this hostel is set in a 200-year-old house with wooden floors and earthy African decor. It has a great location for partying, and is well set up for chilling out. ◎ Map Q4 • 305 Long St • 021 423 7638 • Breakfast excl • www.catandmoose. co.za • R

3 Ashanti Lodge

A place that combines upmarket decor with a relaxed party atmosphere. Good, light meals and chilled drinks are served here. The wide deck has fantastic views of Table Mountain. ◎ Map P6 • 11 Hof St, Gardens • 021 423 8721 • www.ashanti.co.za • RR

4 The Backpack

One of South Africa's oldest backpacker hostels offers more luxurious accommodation along with the standard rooms and dorms. It has a vastly experienced travel centre for excursions. ◎ Map N5 • 74 New Church St, Tamboerskloof • 021 423 4530 • Breakfast excl • www.backpackers.co.za • RR

5 St John's Waterfront Lodge

Set in the inner city suburb of Green Point, this well-established and welcoming hostel is a short walk from the V&A Waterfront (not advisable late at night) and a bus ride from the city. ◎ Map P2 • 6 Braemar Rd, Green Pt • 021 439 1404 • Breakfast excl • www.stjohns. co.za • R

6 Simon's Town Boutique Backpackers

There are surprisingly few good backpackers along the South Peninsula coast. While this is well-positioned for visiting the town and is not far from the Boulders Penguin Colony, it has received mixed reviews. ◎ Map H4 • 66 St George's St • 021 786 1964 • Breakfast excl • www.capepax.co.za • R

7 Stumble Inn

Stumble Inn is located close to historic Dorp Street, and thus convenient for exploring the Stellenbosch CBD. Facilities include a pool and TV lounge. ◎ Map P2 • 12 Market St, Stellenbosch • 021 887 4049 • Breakfast excl • www.stumbleinn backpackers.co.za • R

8 Otter's Bend

Filling a gap in Franschhoek's accommodation scene, this budget hostel has a pretty location. Many outdoor activities can be arranged from here. Eating out is quite costly, but good, in Franschhoek. ◎ Map F2 • Dassenberg Rd, Franschhoek • 021 876 3200 • Breakfast excl • www.ottersbendlodge. co.za • R

9 Hermanus Backpackers

This lively hostel in Hermanus has many types of accommodation and offers activities from caged shark dives at Gansbaai to cliff walks, whale watching and wine tasting along the Walker Bay wine route. ◎ Map U5 • 26 Flower St, Hermanus • 028 312 4293 • www.hermanus backpackers.co.za • R

10 The Beach Camp

The ultimate backpacker hostel for outdoor enthusiasts, this camp offers simple accommodation in tents and A-frames. Other attractions include guided sea kayaking, horse riding, boat trips, snorkelling and walks through the reserve and on the sandy beaches. There is no electricity. ◎ Map S2 • Cape Columbine Nature Reserve, Paternoster • 082 926 2267 • Breakfast excl • www. beachcamp.co.za • R

Almost all backpacker hostels have dormitory accommodation for under R150 per person.

General Index

Acknowledgments

The Author

Born in Britain and raised in Johannesburg, Philip Briggs is the author of more than a dozen travel guides about Africa. He is also a regular contributor to magazines such as Travel Africa, Africa Geographic, Wanderlust and BBC Wildlife.

Photographer
Tony Souter

AT DORLING KINDERSLEY

Publisher
Douglas Amrine

List Manager
Christine Stroyan

Managing Art Editor
Mabel Chan

Senior Editor
Sadie Smith

Project Designers
Paul Jackson
Shahid Mahmood

Senior Cartographic Editor
Casper Morris

Senior Cartographic Designer
Suresh Kumar

Cartographer
Zafarul-Islam Khan

DTP Operator
Natasha Lu

Production
Linda Dare

Fact Checker
Loren Minsky

Revisions
Emma Anacootee, Andrew Baranowski, Claire Baranowski, Madhura Birdi, Louise Cleghorn, Sean Fraser, Carrie Hampton, Mohammad Hassan, Claire Jones, Bharti Karakoti, Sumita Khatwani, Priyanka Kumar, Simon Lewis, Carly Madden, Sam Merrell, Sonal Modha, Ellen Root, Susana Smith, Ajay Verma

Key: a-above; b-below/bottom; c-centre; f-far; l-left; r-right; t-top.

The photographer, writers and publisher would like to thank the media staff at the following sights and organizations for their helpful cooperation:

AGULHAS COUNTRY LODGE: Melanie Cleary 99tl; 118tr.

ALAMY: AfriPics.com 48tl; Fabrice Bettex 55tl; Danita Delimont 36b, 43tl; Danita Delimont/ Cindy Miller Hopkins 92–3; David Sanger Photography 1c; Martin Harvey 12b; Kari Herbert 89tl; Fried von Horsten 40b; Pierre Logwin 34b; Eric Nathan 88tl; Bernard O'Kane 54t; Pictures Colour Library 6ca; Frances Roberts 35tl; Grant Rooney 54br; Steve Allen Travel Photography 18–19c; Peter Titmuss 7bl, 12c, 12cla.

ANNETTE ASHLEY & ASSOCIATES: 68tl.

CITY OF CAPE TOWN: 105tr.

Courtesy of CLIFF LODGE: 118tc.

CORBIS: Franz-Marc Frei 56–7; Gallo Images/Paul Velasco 34tl; John Hicks 28–9c; Hoberman Collection 12–13c; Hulton-Deutsch Collection 34tr; Mark A. Johnson 32–3; Henrik Trygg 49t.

EPA: Nic Bothma 3br, 46br, 48br.

FARR OUT: 118tl.

FOTOLIA: TIG 82tr.

GRAND CAFE & BEACH: 65tl.

GRANDE PROVENCE: 91tl.

IMAGES OF AFRICA: Shaen Adey 40tr, 94cr; Nigel Dennis 97tl; Hein von Horsten 83tr; Lanz von Horsten 3tr, 76tr, 94t; Walter Knirr 77tl, 94cl; Peter Pickford 40c.

IZIKO MUSEUMS OF SOUTH AFRICA SOCIAL HISTORY, SOCIAL HISTORY COLLECTIONS: 17bc.

JONKERSHUIS: 75tl.

JORDAN RESTAURANT: 53tl.

KANONKOP WINE ESTATE: 89tr.

LA COLOMBE: 52tr.

SIMON LEWIS: 6cl, 10cl, 11tl, 109tl, 110tl, 111tr.

MADAME ZINGARA: 67tr.

MEERLUST ESTATE WINE SHOP: 89tl.

RABBIT IN A HAT PR: 112tr.

REUTERS: Howard Burditt 46tc.

RUSTENBERG WINES: 87tl.

SEVRUGA, THE CAVIAR GROUP OF RESTAURANTS: 68tl.

SHIMMY BEACH CLUB: 66tr.

SPIER WINE FARM: 38bl, 90tr.

TERROIR RESTAURANT: 90tl.

VISAGE MEDIA SERVICES: Getty Images/Frans Lemmens 24–5c.

IAN WEBB: 49br.

ZULU SOUND BAR: 66tc.

Map Cover: SIMON LEWIS.

Special Editions of DK Travel Guides

DK Travel Guides can be purchased in bulk quantities at discounted prices for use in promotions or as premiums. We are also able to offer special editions and personalized jackets, corporate imprints and excerpts from all of our books, tailored specifically to meet your own needs.

To find out more, please contact:

(in the United States) **SpecialSales@dk.com**

(in the UK) **TravelSpecialSales@uk.dk.com**

(in Canada) DK Special Sales at **general@tourmaline.ca**

(in Australia) **business.development@pearson.com.au**

Selected Street and Towns Index

Selected Street and Towns Index